D1369998

MONEY MATTERS MADE EASY

The Q & A reference for everything from
Asset Allocation to **Z**ero-Coupon Bonds

By Steven C. Camp

TRUNKEY PUBLISHING COMPANY

MONEY MATTERS MADE EASY

Copyright 1997 by Steven C. Camp
Library Congress Card No. 97-61406

Cataloging-in-Publication Data

332.024   Camp, Steven C. (Steven Charles), 1941 Dec. 9-
CAM   Money matters made easy : the Q & A reference for everything from
          asset allocation to zero-coupon bonds / by Steven C. Camp. - Ft. Lauderdale,
          Fla. : Trunkey Publishing Co., 1997.

              160 p.; 21 cm.
              Includes index.

              Summary: Provides answers to common financial questions, with special
          emphasis on how the market works for investors. Includes information on
          increasing income, cutting taxes, and planning for retirement.

              ISBN 1-88760-01-X

              1. Finance, Personal - Questions and answers 2. Saving and investment -
          Questions and answers I. Title

          HG179   332.024_dc21

              Provided in cooperation with Unique Books, Inc.

Published by
Trunkey Publishing Company
2841 NE 21st Court
Fort Lauderdale, FL 33305-3617

Printed in the United States of America

DEDICATION

To the memory of my parents, Lilo and Erwin Camp.

To my wife, Melanie, and our daughters, Elizabeth and Stephanie, for their love, support and assistance.

To my friend, Rick Silverman, who encouraged and persuaded me to change careers and become a financial consultant with a major brokerage firm.

To the thousands of individuals who attended my Informed Investor Seminars. Their questions formed the basis of this book.

ALSO BY STEVEN C. CAMP

**MONEY: 127 Answers
To Your Most-Asked Financial Questions**

Contents

Acknowledgments

For publicizing and arranging Informed Investor Seminars at bookstores and libraries: Michael Agrifolio, Greg Barnett, Peter Bernard, Susan Boyd, Tara Brock, Georgina Cardenas, Oline Cogdill, Darlene Combs, Teri Connolly, Joe Donzelli, Vicki Feffe, Sherry Friedlander, Luz Garcia, Verna Greene, John Helmus, Frank Herrera, Constance Houck, Scott Hutchinson, Christine Jones, Lindsay Koehler, Judy Martin, Stephanie Silton, Tanya Simons-Oprah, Yzaura Vanegas-Andino, Bob Weaver, Myra Weaver, Susan Yarab, Terie Yarboro, and Barbara Young.

I wish to acknowledge our editors, Ellen Guest of New York City and David Kohn of Deerfield Beach, Florida, along with Betty Wright and Betsy Lampé of Rainbow Books. Their suggestions were invaluable in transforming manuscript notes into book form.

Special thanks for checking the accuracy of the contents to Bruce Beardslee, James Benedek, Mary-Lee Carey, Victor Fier, Harold Johnson, Ralph Leach, Chris Miller, Bob McCabe, Delores Mulligan, Jeff Pawliger, Steve Pawliger, Bob Peffers, Douglas Schindewolf, Sandy Schmidt, Steve Sciaretta, and Joe Scott.

Introduction

Dear Investor:

As a financial consultant who conducts numerous public seminars nationwide in major bookstores, I was surprised to discover a common need among investors that is not being well addressed. It's a need for basic information about financial planning and investing.

When I conduct seminars, I begin by asking everyone to tell me the questions they would most like answered. This book is made up of many of those questions along with my answers. It simply offers brief and basic answers to money questions you and millions of people like you face.

My clients know I believe strongly that being an informed investor is crucial to long-term financial success. I also recommend that investors work with a professional financial consultant. Together, you make a team dedicated to a single mission: defining your specific financial goals and then achieving them. But remember: *nobody cares about your money as much as you do.* You need to become an educated investor if you wish to attain your long-term financial goals.

This book will help get you started. My purpose here is not to cover every aspect of investing the way an encyclopedia might. There are other books on the market that do just that. What I want to do is provide some basic information about the kind of real, day-to-day questions concerning money that you and I face again and again. You'll also learn who I recommend that you read in the press and watch on television to keep and stay informed.

After reading through these pages, you may very well find that you have a question about something I haven't covered. *I invite you to communicate directly with me.* I'll try to answer your questions promptly to the best of my ability. My telephone number is 954-561-6515 or fax: 954-565-8609.

Wishing you a prosperous future,

Steven C. Camp

Chapter **1**

Evaluating Investments

Structuring an investment portfolio is an individual matter. Each investor has his or her own unique financial goals, tolerance for risk, time frame, investment experience, and amount of money he or she wishes to commit. Your portfolio should be the product of a well-executed investment plan that you've reached by consulting with professionals who are thoroughly familiar with your personal circumstances and expectations.

Many of the questions and concerns voiced at my "Informed Investor" seminars deal with the exasperation of investors who are attempting to structure their portfolios. The source of this frustration is the vast number of options investors must choose from. However, when you manage risk through diversification and asset allocation, and maintain a long-term perspective while still focusing on short-term needs, your investment journey will be smoother and less stressful. And, when you look back after reaching your goal, the trip will have been worth it.

What are your most important long-range goals? Building wealth? Total financial independence? Planning for retirement or college for your children and grandchildren? As your personal situation changes, so may your investment objectives.

Realize that you are the author of your plan for financial security, and you can modify your plan as your long-term prospects change.

1

With all the different investment choices available, how can I select the best one?

First determine how much money you need to accumulate by a certain date to accomplish your financial goal. Don't forget to factor in a certain rate for inflation. Based upon your time horizon and tolerance for risk, you will be able to narrow your investment choices and select those with which you are most comfortable. A competent investment adviser, financial planner or broker should be able to suggest suitable investments.

2

How can I screen out inaccurate information when I'm using the Internet?

By cross-checking. The Internet has allowed investors to get information about current and potential investments. But faster information doesn't mean better information, or even information that's as good. Some Internet sites have information from well-established organizations you can rely upon; but many sites are not so reputable. You must check Internet financial information against sources which already have proven reliable, such as an investment professional and financial publications.

3

I understand the need to be diversified. I'm invested in four different mutual funds. Is this being diversified?

It may not be. Many times individuals invest in three different diversified funds hoping that these funds will provide the variety they need to spread their risk, but upon careful examination, we can see that the major holdings of each of these funds are practically identical. So in the guise of diversifying they have triplicated their portfolios and not really achieved their goal. Diversification means not putting all of your investment eggs in one basket. If the basket falls, you've not only lost your investments, but also the time benefit of compounding.

4

How do I measure risk when evaluating an investment?

There are major causes of risk.

◆ **Volatility** describes the tendency of an investment to suddenly shift in value from high to low or from low to high.

The more volatile an investment is, the greater profit you can earn. That's because there is a bigger potential spread between the price you pay for it and its market price when you sell it.

◆ **Demanding high yield** describes when the economy is down and interest rates decline, many investors still expect the same rate of return, and seek investments of lesser quality in order to achieve it. Seeking a higher return can result in higher losses as well.

◆ **Playing it too safe** describes the more money you have

in the safest investments (like CDs, bank accounts, and treasury bills), the smaller your chances are for substantial rewards. When you play it too safe, there is always the risk of outliving your assets because they won't keep up with inflation.

5

Are volatility and risk the same?

No. **Volatility** is a two-way street. A volatile investment tends to go up or down more than the market as a whole does. Examples of investments that tend to be volatile are long-term treasury bonds and zero-coupon bonds. As interest rates rise, the value of these investments will decrease. As interest rates drop, the value goes up. Market risk is the downside of volatility.

Liquidity risk is a concern for an investor who is planning to use the proceeds of the sale of an investment for another purpose (paying for a child's tuition, his/her income taxes, the closing costs of a new residence, etc.).

Almost all of us have seen the effects of liquidity risk among people who have lost their jobs, been faced with divorces, or need to relocate when there seems to be no market for their current homes.

6

Am I better off investing in stocks or bonds? Which is safer?

It depends upon your investment objectives — whether you are looking for short-term or long-term gains. If you look at the chart provided by Ibbotson Associates, you will see the performance of stocks and bonds over a 70-year period. Obviously, stocks have done much better.

Which are safer? Bonds used to be safer than stocks; but in 1994, the volatility of the bond market made investing in a mixture of stocks and bonds less risky than investing only in bonds.

7

As a retiree, how can I maintain my income without losing purchasing power?

This is a dilemma confronting many retirees. Do you realize that, considering today's increasing life spans, it's possible to spend more time being retired than you spent working? If we look at the Ibbotson chart and we see the different performance of stocks, bonds, and Treasury bills over seventy years, we realize that retirees who put their savings in bonds and certificates of deposit will lose a lot of their purchasing power and will not be able to keep up with inflation. So you need to anticipate not only income needs but also growth needs. That way, your portfolio will grow faster than the rate of inflation, and you will be able to maintain your purchasing power during retirement without being in danger of outliving your savings.

Compound Annual Rate of Return, 1925 - 1996

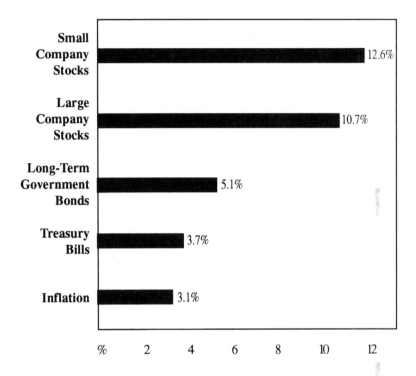

8

Can you explain "asset allocation?"

"Asset allocation" is the process of determining which classes of assets to invest in. For example, you may invest 50% in stocks, 25% in bonds, and 25% in cash money market, so the asset allocation would be referred to as "50, 25, 25." The way you allocate your assets determines the return over the long run for your individual portfolio. In 91% of cases studied, asset allocation was the key influence on portfolio returns.

Components of Investment Return

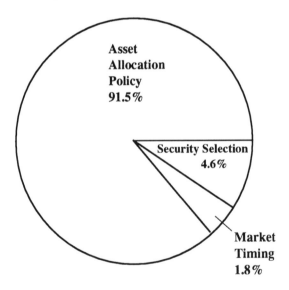

Source: © *The Asset Allocation Decision* Presentation 1990-1997. Ibbotson Associates, Chicago. Used with permission. All rights reserved.

9

What is the difference between rate-of-return and real rate-of-return?

As an investor, the true test is not what you make on your investments but what you get to *keep* after inflation and taxes. Let's assume you have invested in a CD that is returning 5.5%. What is your *real* rate of return?

Total return	=	5.50%
less 28% federal tax	=	-1.54%
less Inflation	=	-4.00%
Real rate of return	=	- .04%

10

You mentioned the need to be diversified in order to minimize risk. How many stocks do I need to own to be diversified enough?

Although that answer will be different for each investor, the benefits of diversification level off when there are more than ten stocks in a portfolio. Take a look at this diagram:

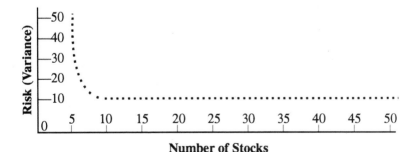

Number of Stocks

11

What is the difference between closed-end and open-end funds? Which is better?

An open-end fund is a mutual fund. Open-end funds issue additional shares when all shares have been purchased. When shares are cashed in or sold, open-end funds redeem these shares and then cancel them. Closed-end funds have initial offerings of a limited number of shares. It's very similar to a stock issue. The price is determined solely by the market. The price of closed-end funds can be more or less than the net asset value.

Which is better? It depends upon your objectives. Usually a closed-end fund invests in a specific sector or geographic region (such as technology or Latin America). With an open-end mutual fund, you can transfer from one fund to another within a family of funds without incurring a sales charge. This transfer of funds is a taxable event unless it occurs within a retirement account or variable annuity.

12

What is the difference between a unit trust and a mutual fund?

Unit trusts and mutual funds are investment companies. They provide investors an opportunity to benefit from professional management, liquidity and diversification.

Unit trusts issue only redeemable securities that are fixed for the life of a trust. The portfolio remains unchanged once the unit trust is established and it does not need to be managed. It is supervised whereas a mutual fund has an indefinite life. Since a mutual fund is constantly buying and selling securities within its portfolios, it is managed. In Britain, unit trust is the name given to what Americans call an open-end mutual fund.

13

What are sector funds?

Sector funds are mutual and closed-end funds that concentrate their investments within a specific industry. Such industries include natural resources, banking, financial services, gold, science and technology. Other sector funds specialize either in geographic regions (such as Latin America or the Pacific Rim), or individual nations (such as Mexico or Korea). Sector funds let an investor pinpoint industries or regions offering outstanding growth potential. These investments don't offer diversification, so they tend to be more volatile.

When TV financial commentators discuss the "relative performance" of a sector, usually they are measuring the performance of a specific sector index divided by the Standard & Poors 500 Index. Remember: normally when the Federal Reserve Board raises interest rates, the Financial Sector Index drops more than the S&P 500 index. That's because individual financial sectors are very interest rate sensitive.

14

Isn't it more economical to buy no-load mutual funds because you don't have to pay any fees?

It's a misconception that "no-load" means "no fees," even though many no-load mutual funds maintain toll-free numbers for shareholders and produce elegant brochures. The cost for these services are paid by shareholders in fees. The "no-load" means you'll pay no-sales load or sales commission.

Historically, no-load mutual fund shareholders tend to switch out of their funds more quickly than owners of "load" funds. This is because the sales charge acts as an incentive not to bail out at the first market downturn. No-load mutual funds have a much higher redemption rate than "load" mutual funds. When investors start to try to time the market, they usually penalize themselves by buying high and selling low.

Most investors are better off buying a mutual fund and holding it for the long-run, rather than redeeming shares at a downturn and buying more at an upturn.

15

Is there a difference between global funds and international funds?

Yes. Global funds invest in the stocks of companies throughout the world — including those of the United States. International funds invest in the stocks of companies outside the United States and its domestic economy.

More and more, we hear about America being part of the global economy, and about American workers and firms having to compete in the global economy. U.S. businesses, both small and large, have been adapting to this global economy by restructuring their assets, personnel and marketing focuses. Many American companies and brands are accepted by consumers worldwide.

In the same way, many foreign companies have plants in the United States and their products are widely accepted by American consumers.

The world is becoming smaller because of a global economy that provides mutual benefits through increased trade and improved standards of living. Today, nations have more of an incentive to get along economically, and therefore need to maintain harmonious relations. Can you imagine a business offending or upsetting an important customer? The same holds true for nations dependent upon each other for their economic well-being.

16

I'd like to diversify my portfolio through overseas investments. Which do you recommend: developed markets like Western Europe and Japan or emerging markets like Latin America and Asia?

According to Morgan Stanley Capital International, the average annual rate of return for 1986-1996 (in U.S. dollars with gross dividends reinvested) was 22.06% in emerging markets and only 10.58% in developed markets. The highest growth rates are found in emerging markets. The P/E (price-earnings) ratio is generally lower in emerging markets (reflecting a better value).

I suggest you consult your financial advisor about investing in an emerging market fund with a solid track record. Some of the possible risks of investing in emerging markets that are not encountered in U.S. funds are fluctuation in currencies, restrictions on foreign investment, the possibility of exchange controls, less publicly available data, less liquidity, and differences in government regulation and supervision. There also may be concerns about political instability, hyperinflation, and market instability.

17

I've heard a lot about the attractive returns from overseas investing, but it sounds risky. Can I benefit from overseas investing by buying stock in blue chip American companies?

Yes. Foreign sales represent an average of 43% of total sales for the thirty companies comprising the Dow Jones Industrial Average (shown below). The percentage of sales from international sources ranges from a low of 1% for Travelers to 80%

for Exxon.

The source for these figures is each company's investor relations, media or public relations department and their annual reports. These figures represent the most recent data available as of August 1, 1996.

Company	Stock Symbol	Percentage of International Sales
AT&T	T	26%
Allied Signal	ALD	37%
Aluminum Co. of America	AA	44%
American Express	AXP	29%
Johnson & Johnson	JNJ	50%
Boeing	BA	52%
Caterpillar	CAT	52%
Chevron	CHV	33%
Coca-Cola	KO	71%
Disney	DIS	23%
DuPont	DD	47%
Eastman Kodak	EK	54%
Exxon	XON	80%
General Electric	GE	38%
General Motors	GM	19%
Goodyear	GT	45%
IBM	IBM	63%
International Paper	IP	36%
McDonalds	MCD	54%
Merck	MRK	31%
3M	MMM	54%
JP Morgan	JPM	51%
Philip Morris	MO	54%
Proctor Gamble	PG	53%
Sears	S	11%
Hewlett-Packard	HWP	50%
Union Carbide	UK	31%
United Technologies	UTX	55%
Travelers	TRV	1%
Wal-Mart	WMT	37%

Average International Sales   43%

18

Won't I get a better return by investing in a no-load mutual fund since I will not be charged a sales commission?

A study of investor behavior was conducted by DALBAR Financial Services of Boston and published in April 1994. DALBAR studied 1,000 mutual fund investors for almost ten years. (This is called the Quantitative Analysis of Investor Behavior.) The study measured the average returns that these 1,000 investors received to determine if investors who pay a sales load and receive advice from a financial consultant enjoyed better, equal, or worse returns than no-load investors do. DALBAR's findings were:

1. Equity mutual fund investors who used a financial consultant outperformed no-load investors by 19%.
2. Fixed-income fund investors who used a financial consultant outperformed no-load investors by 17%.

According to DALBAR, "investors who do not seek advice were more likely to panic and sell when the market dived. With the advice and knowledge of a financial consultant available when market conditions are volatile, clients were more likely to hold on to their investments during market downturns."

Many investors who claim to be long-term investors sell at the first downturn. Without someone steady to reassure them that this negative situation is only temporary, investors do not reap the benefit of stable, long-term investments.

19

What is the "contrarian" investment philosophy?

When everyone else seems to look with disfavor upon an investment, contrarians start to buy it. In order to "buy low, sell high" you have to buy in adverse times and sell in robust times. When a company reports disappointing earnings (causing investors to dump a stock), contrarians view this unfavorable event as a potential buying opportunity.

20

What about investing in commodities?

If you are able to invest in high risk investments such as commodities and can afford to lose the money without it affecting you, your lifestyle, or your retirement plan, then go ahead and invest in high risk investments. But if you can't afford to lose any principal or find it too stressful to lose money, then do not invest in high risk investments like commodities and options.

21

What are derivatives? Are they a good investment?

Derivatives are financial investments whose value is derived from another security. An **option** is one type of derivative. The value of an option is derived from the value of the underlying stock. Derivatives enables the investor to have considerable leverage. By investing in derivatives, the returns are much greater in up-markets, but the risks are worse in down markets. But leverage works both ways. When the markets go down, you can lose everything very quickly.

Many professional investors who have been very successful in good times have incurred major losses when the market turned against them, because they invested in derivatives. Remember: *There is no free lunch.* There is a definite relationship between risk and reward.

22

What percentage of my portfolio should be invested in precious metals such as gold and silver?

During the early part of the 1980s, when we experienced double-digit inflation, precious metal investments were heavily promoted as hedges against inflation. In the 1990s, however, there's been little inflation and precious metals have been a horrible investment. They've even lost money. With no visible signs of inflation, I would not recommend investing in precious metals.

23

Any suggestions for a person who wins the lottery?

First of all, it is vital that you tell no one of your winnings, because your life will change dramatically and immediately if you do. You will most likely be besieged by people soliciting you for causes and investments you never dreamed of. By maintaining an extremely low profile, you can avoid being taken advantage of.

Another good idea is to change your telephone number and have it unlisted. Do not sign the winning ticket until after you have met with your attorney because there can only be one name on the winning ticket. It may be advisable to name as the winner a trust or partnership suggested by your attorney.

Meet with an attorney as soon as possible and set up a trust agreement or partnership so that you can minimize the tax effects of receiving a large sum of money. It is crucial for you to meet with some professionals so that you make the right moves with your new-found wealth.

If you have a winning lottery ticket, it is essential that you safeguard it. Put it in a safe place and tell only those you trust of its location.

There was a $17+ million lottery winner in Melbourne, Florida, on September 4, 1993. She owned a local beauty salon and her husband was an air force sergeant. This woman told no one about her winning ticket, not even her spouse or grown children. She put it in a bank safe deposit for safekeeping. At Christmas, she gave her husband a gift-wrapped present containing this winning ticket. But that could have been a big mistake. If she had become ill or incapacitated, the expiration date could have passed (six months and one day after the date on that winning ticket) and the ticket would have become worthless.

In 1996, more than 120 people were struck by lightning in Florida and less than 40 people won the lottery. A Florida resident is more than three times more likely to be struck by lightning than to win the lottery.

24

I have an investment account that is managed by the trust department of a major bank. Most of my assets are in municipal bonds, and the rest is in stocks that I've owned for many years. I cannot afford to sell them because of the capital gains taxes that I would have to pay. Should I maintain this account even though I have to pay approximately one percent on the value of my assets in this account annually, and also approximately one percent on any income I receive from this account?

If you are maintaining an investment account at the trust department of a bank and the account is being warehoused or stored, you may want to reevaluate the account's cost structure with the person handling your account at the bank. You may be in an excellent position to renegotiate your fee structure if there are no transactions within your account and your account is static. That same account in a brokerage firm would not be charged a set percentage fee just to store municipal bonds and securities.

25

Am I better off using a mutual fund or professional money manager for my "serious money"? What are the benefits of one versus the other?

There is no right answer here. A lot depends upon the amount of money you have to invest, your risk tolerance and your investment experience. Your individual expectations and comfort level are important, too.

Most professional money managers have a $100,000 minimum account size and specialize in one discipline. (For example, their expertise might be in a specific size of company, value or growth investments, income investing, etc.) Remember, your portfolio needs three or more disciplines to allocate your assets in a balanced fashion.

Mutual fund investors are a part of a large group and they can't usually contact their portfolio manager. They also could end up with big tax and no gain if they invest in a fund late in the year. That's when funds generally pay out all their capital gains, on which all fund investors must pay tax. If their fund then goes down, those investors have paid tax and taken a loss too.

Mutual fund managers, especially those of no-load funds are truly at the mercy of their shareholders. When the markets drop, shareholders become scared and cash in. So fund managers must then sell stocks to pay those shareholders and miss a buying opportunity. Conversely, when markets reach new highs and money pours into the fund, managers have to buy while they are paying ever-higher prices.

A professional money manager has none of these pressures because each account is managed individually. You can even specify industries and companies you wish to avoid.

26

What type of investment do socially responsible mutual funds avoid?

Socially responsible mutual fund managers avoid investing in companies involved in tobacco production, military weapons production, nuclear utilities and manufacturers/distributors of unsafe products. These managers believe that shareholders benefit by investing in socially responsible companies that have much lower legal costs and superior images. Many labor unions, religious groups, teacher pension funds, health care organizations and individuals feel an ethical imperative to invest in a socially responsible manner consistent with their core beliefs.

27

How much do you recommend I maintain in cash for quick access? I am 63 years old.

A good rule-of-thumb is to maintain three to six months' worth of living expenses in cash or money market funds. As one becomes older, there is a tendency to maintain larger amounts in cash. You should maintain an amount that you feel comfortable having in cash. However, some retirees take this to an extreme and maintain two to three years' worth of living expenses in cash or money market. It's probably not a good idea to maintain this much money in cash or money market funds because it will not grow as fast as the rate of inflation.

28

Could you explain the "Rule of 72"?

The *Rule of 72* is used by investors to compute the amount of time it will take for an investment to double in value. If you take the rate of return you want and divide it into the number 72, the result will be the number of years it takes for the investment to double. For example, if you assume an investment will have an 8% rate of return (compounded annually), divide 72 by 8. Since 72 divided by 8 equals nine, it will take approximately nine years for that investment to double.

If you divide the number of years it takes for an investment to double into 72, you will get the compounded annual rate of return. For example, if you could double an investment in five years, and you divide five into 72, the result is about 14 plus percent (compounded annually).

Many people are fascinated by this rule. It works in the same way that 3.14 (pi) works in computing the area or circumference of a circle.

Chapter 2

Brokerage Firms

Most Americans feel financial pressures from all sides and also feel that their personal financial situations have not improved during the past five years. Its also true that most Americans do not have clear financial plans. By developing a realistic financial plan and paying yourself first, you will be in a better position to achieve your goals. Seek the assistance of a competent financial professional to advise you on investment choices that suit your expectations and tolerance for risk.

Since I am associated with a major brokerage firm, many of the questions asked at my seminars are about whether or not to have a broker, how to find a "good broker," the problems that may occur if your broker goes out of business, and the ways an investor can use the professional services of a brokerage firm.

When you visit your accountant or tax-preparer, what type of client are you?

Do you drop off a shoe box or shopping bag full of last year's receipts with the expectation that they will be sorted, compiled and used in preparing your tax returns?

or

Do you have last year's income and expense files neatly prepared and documented so that your records are easy to follow and are self explanatory?

Many people realize that they have neither the time, energy, inclination nor financial expertise to act as money managers. So, they seek the services of a professional. These investors are not giving up control of their investments; they are using a broker as a financial consultant or investment advisor. In this age of specialization, it usually pays to "do what you do best and hire out the rest."

Successful people know how to use "OPB" ("other people's brains"). If you are a biologist, automobile dealer, orchestra cellist or realtor, then how are you going to find the time, money and energy to be a do-it-yourself money manager?

29

How do you find a good broker?

Much the same way you'd find a good lawyer, a good accountant, a good doctor, or a good mechanic. Ask friends and people you trust. Find out what they value about that person, and use that information to make your decision. Then meet with that person and discover if he or she is compatible with you. Does his or her viewpoint of the economy and market make sense to you? Does he or she understand your risk tolerance? Your investment objectives? Are the levels of expectations for each of you in harmony? Also, does he or she fully answer the questions that you ask? Is that person condescending or patronizing to you? If so, you will want to work with someone else.

30

What do you think of investment clubs?

I like them. You probably will too. Any activity that makes you better informed and more comfortable about investing will benefit you.

By becoming an active member of an investment club, you and your fellow members will learn from each other. If you want to learn about the principles of investing, I recommend that you join one. (Here's a tip: make sure you are compatible with the other members.) It's an enjoyable way to learn about the do's and don'ts of investing. It's also a lot less expensive than the trial and error method of losing while learning.

For investment club information, write or call the National

Association of Investment Clubs (NAIC) at 711 West Thirteen Mile Road, Madison Heights, Michigan, 48071. Tel: 810-583-6242 Fax: 810-583-4880. Approximately one-half of the investment clubs in the United States are affiliated with NAIC.

31

I get a monthly brokerage account statement and I do not know how to read it. What suggestions do you have for helping me to understand my statement?

Many clients do not understand their monthly statements and are reluctant to ask for help. (They also may not check their checking account statements from their local banks each month.) Meet with your financial consultant and have him or her explain your entire brokerage account statement so that you fully understand it. If there is any part of the statement that you don't understand, make sure it is explained to you.

If you are not comfortable approaching your financial consultant, you can speak to his or her customer service assistant and have that person explain it to you. You owe it to yourself to understand the monthly statement from your brokerage firm because you are ultimately responsible for what happens in your account. It's your money!

32

I have an account at a brokerage firm and I like my broker a lot. However, I read stories in the newspapers about brokers who embezzle money from their customers. How can I protect myself against being ripped off?

First, never forget that no one cares about your money as much as you. Get involved in understanding your financial affairs — do not delegate this responsibility completely to a broker, financial advisor, accountant, friend, family member, or even your spouse. You are responsible for:

1. Reading and understanding your statements, and looking for errors or omissions. Ask your broker or branch operations manager to explain anything you do not understand.
2. Examining your trade confirmations to make sure they are accurate. File your statements in a loose leaf notebook separated by month or quarter, and look for any changes in security positions.

To check whether a broker has been disciplined by a regulatory agency or by the NASD in the past, call the NASD toll-free hotline at 1-800-289-9999. To find out if the firm is a member of SIPC (Securities Investor Protection Corporation) call SIPC-1-202-371-8300. All brokers and dealers registered with the SEC and with national stock exchanges are required to be members. The SIPC insures customers' accounts in case the firm fails. The overall maximum is $500,000 per customer, with a limit of $100,000 in cash or cash equivalents. In addition to the $500,000 protection provided by SIPC, some firms provide additional insurance. SIPC does not provide insurance against market risks.

33

I get bombarded with annoying telephone calls from brokers who are trying to sell me the latest stock or bond of the day. They usually call around dinner time. Is there anything I can do to be removed from these cold-calling lists?

Yes, there is. For instance, if you live in Florida and don't wish to receive sales solicitation calls, get your name added to the "No Sales Solicitation Calls" list maintained by the Florida Department of Consumer Services. (Call the Division of Consumer Services at 1-800-HELP-FLA.) The list is updated quarterly. For a $5 fee, your number will remain on the list for one year. Businesses that solicit calls from numbers on this list can be fined $10,000. In other states, call the State Attorney General's office or the Department of Consumer Affairs.

34

What can I do so that my name is removed from mailing lists so that I do not receive offers, solicitations, magazines, promotional contests and pre-approved credit card applications?

Request in writing that your name be removed from mailing lists from any organizations soliciting you. Consumers may also write:

Direct Marketing Association
Mail Preference Service
P.O. Box 9008
Farmingdale, NY 11735-90008

Trans Union Corporations Name Removal Option
P.O. Box 7245
Fullerton, California 92637

35

What are the pros and cons of placing my securities in a brokerage firm's vault versus keeping them in my safe deposit box?

Many people are reluctant to put securities in a brokerage firm's vault. By leaving them in their own safe deposit boxes, they feel they're safer and under their own control. Unfortunately, many securities are misplaced this way. And if you ever lose a stock certificate or a bond, it is a problem to replace it. Also, if you become incapacitated, ill, or die, then access to the securities in the safe deposit box may become very difficult — or even denied — in certain states.

Securities placed in a brokerage firm's vault are insured by the SIPC (Securities Investor Protection Corporation) for up to $500,000. Some firms also carry additional insurance for their clients' accounts. Securities held at a brokerage firm are probably safer and easier to track than securities held in a safe deposit box.

Many retirees are not enjoying their retirements because they are spending 2-3 or more hours daily managing their investments. Much unnecessary paperwork could easily be computerized and done more accurately by a brokerage firm.

36

I've misplaced a stock certificate. What should I do?

"You lose, you pay" is the best way to describe this situation. You must contact the transfer agent. You can get the name and number from your broker or the investor relations department of the company whose stock you own.

The agent will start a *stop transfer* which lets brokerages and others know that this certificate can't be transferred to any person or institution. In that respect, it's like putting a *stop payment* on a check.

The agent will also tell you that you must buy a surety bond. Here's where you pay. That bond protects the agent against the risk of the missing certificate somehow being reissued. The premium, which comes out of your pocket, is about 2 percent of the certificate's face value. The transfer agent will have the forms so you can obtain a surety bond.

If you lost a registered bond, follow the same procedure as for a lost stock certificate. If you've lost a U.S. savings bond, call (804) 697-8370 to reach the U.S. Savings Bond Division of the U.S. Treasury Department.

37

What is the difference between the *prime rate* and the *discount rate*? Or are they the same?

No. They're not the same. The **discount rate** is the interest rate that the Federal Reserve charges member banks when those banks borrow money using government securities as collateral. The raising or lowering of the discount rate is one of the tools the Federal Reserve uses to try to stimulate the economy or to reduce inflationary pressures.

The **prime rate** is the interest rate that banks charge for loans to their most creditworthy customers. It is considered a key benchmark because other rates are tied into it. For example, the interest rate for many credit cards (home equity loan and automobile leases) is based upon the prime rate plus a set number of percentage points.

38

What happens if my broker becomes bankrupt? Are my securities protected?

If your brokerage firm is a member of the Securities Investors Protection Corporation (SIPC), the account is insured for balances up to $500,000. Ask your broker for information.

39

How would you describe an ideal investor or client?

An ideal investor does five things:

1. Is willing to invest without procrastinating.
2. Consistently adds to his/her account.
3. Communicates clearly his/her risk tolerance, and has reasonable expectations.
4. Expects the market to fluctuate, and takes advantage of any fluctuations via dollar cost averaging.
5. Doesn't get discouraged when things get tough. That means having the long-term perspective to ride the ups and downs of the market, and not selling at the first down-turn.

40

How can I be more knowledgeable about investing so I don't need a broker?

Without being facetious, all you need to do is have as much knowledge, judgment, and up-to-date information as a competent full-time broker or adviser. In addition, you need to be willing and able to spend 40-50 hours weekly managing and monitoring your investments.

Obviously, if you're asking this question, you have reason to feel that the commissions you have paid in the past to a brokerage firm or broker have not been justly earned by that broker or firm.

41

How do I calculate my net worth?

Your net worth is determined by constructing a balance sheet that lists your assets (what you own) and your liabilities (what you owe). The difference between the two represents your net worth.

Your bank can give you a "Statement of Net Worth" form that is used by loan applicants. Fill in values for assets using the appropriate market value (not your cost price). Separate your assets by liquid and non-liquid investments. (Retirement plan assets such as 401(k) plans are considered non-liquid assets.)

42

What kind of questions should my financial advisor be asking me when we meet for the first time? What should I tell him or her?

Some of the questions your financial advisor should be asking you deal with your objectives for investing: the reasons you are investing, the level of risk that you are able to assume, and the amount of money you have to invest. Remember that your financial advisor is a consultant. In order to help you, he or she needs as much information as possible about your expectations, your prior investment experience, your assets and liabilities, and your time horizon. This person should treat everything you say as confidential — you need to be clear about that with this person before divulging any information.

Here's what you should tell your investment advisor: everything he or she needs to understand about your finances (including your prior investment successes, disappointments and expectations). If you have accounts held at other firms, let this person know. If you or members of your family have any major health or interpersonal problems, your financial advisor may need to know this information. This way he or she will be able to better advise you about health and estate planning matters.

43

How does a discretionary account work?

In a discretionary account, you authorize a financial consultant or broker to make investment decisions without consulting you first. The broker has the authority (or "discretion") to buy or sell investments that he or she thinks are in your best interest.

44

I am 74 years old and have accounts at three brokerage firms. Do you advise that I consolidate these three accounts into one?

I recommend that you do whatever you feel most comfortable doing. If you can manage three different accounts, and each of the accounts is enabling you to achieve your investment objectives, there may be no need to consolidate them. However, many investors who maintain different accounts may be creating a tremendous amount of unnecessary paperwork for themselves.

If you are one of these people, consolidate your investments with the financial advisor with whom you feel most comfortable and believe is most able to help you obtain your objectives. Remember, it is important for you to streamline your portfolio and eliminate unnecessary paperwork while you're in good health. Can you imagine the hassles and added expenses that your loved ones will have trying to unravel your affairs if you are not able to help them?

Chapter 3

Economic Influences

It is estimated that two-thirds of all Americans do not pay their Visa or MasterCard bills in full when they receive them. Many simply make the minimum payment and let the annual interest charges of 18% plus escalate.

Interest rate charges for consumer debt are no longer tax deductible. This means that people in the 28% tax bracket must earn 25% *before taxes* to be able to afford to pay 18% in interest charges *after taxes* for their credit card debt. Where can you find an investment guaranteed to pay you a 25% annual return? Eliminate your credit card debt and you will have avoided a minus 25% annual drain on your assets.

Many investors feel that the greatest risk to their portfolios is economic and financial volatility. It is not. *Inflation* is the greatest risk.

If inflation averages 4% annually, how much will your purchasing power shrink?

After 5 years of 4% inflation, the value of $1 is just 82 cents

10 years,	the value of $1	66 cents
15 years,	the value of $1	54 cents
20 years,	the value of $1	44 cents
25 years,	the value of $1	36 cents

This means that a 4% annual inflation rate will reduce the purchasing power of $100,000 as follows:

Number of years	Purchasing power
5 years	$82,000
10 years	$66,000
15 years	$54,000
20 years	$44,000
25 years	$36,000
30 years	$30,000

As we examine these figures (assuming that inflation will only average 4% annually), today's retiree will need to double his or her income every 18 years to maintain the same standard of living he or she currently enjoys.

45

I watch *Wall Street Week* every Friday on PBS and enjoy it. However, I'm totally confused after seeing this panel of experts disagree — some are bearish and others are bullish. Do you have any suggestions for making sense of all of this?

These days we have a surplus of information — and much of that information is contradictory. It is very confusing to hear one expert give cogent reasons for the economy to perform in a certain way and then hear another expert argue forcefully about why the economy is likely to move in the opposite direction. The credentials of each expert are apt to be very impressive, and this only adds to the frustration.

I sympathize. And I am reminded of a recent year-end *Wall Street Week* program. Each of the guests on the show was dressed formally as if he or she were attending a New Year's Eve Party. The host reviewed each expert's predictions for the past year and then invited them to predict the highs and lows of the Dow Jones Industrials for the next 12 months. The variation among the guests in predicting the year-end for the Dow varied by more than 1,000 points.

We need to keep these short-term views in perspective. The truth is, smart investors take a long-range view and invest for the long-run. If you invest over the long run in solid companies and solid investments, then the minor ups and downs of the market (and of the opinions of commentators) have a minimal impact on your portfolio.

Here are some rules for long-term success: Invest in companies that are leaders in their industries and that enjoy a 15% or greater annual increase in earnings over the past five years. Reinvest the dividends. Companies that are able to increase their earnings consistently regardless of the economy are usually well-run. Avoid being enticed by "bargains" in the stock market that offer "a quick killing." Review your monthly financial statements, and do not worry about monitoring your investments every day. Remember, you're in it for the long run.

46

What is the difference between fiscal and monetary policies?

The federal government is responsible for fiscal policy and the Federal Reserve, a quasi-governmental organization, is responsible for monetary policy or the availability of credit. The Federal Reserve works to loosen or tighten credit by changing the interest rates, the reserve requirements and the money supply. Fiscal policy includes how federal and local governments tax and spend money.

47

Whenever there is a negative economic report (like an increase in unemployment), the stock market seems to go up. Why is bad news good for the stock market?

Wall Street has a tremendous fear of inflation. When reports say that the economy is doing well, analysts fear that the economy will be heating up and that inflation will start to rise. Since that tends to have long-term negative effects upon the stock market, analysts tend to agree that the Federal Reserve will have to step in and raise interest rates. The Fed may also reduce the economy's money supply. This tends to slow the economy and prevent expansion — and can almost create a recession. This has a detrimental effect upon the stock market in the long run.

When there is economic bad news (which indicates that the economy is growing slowly or not at all), then the Federal Reserve is likely to stimulate the economy by encouraging businesses to borrow by lowering interest rates. This has a positive effect upon the stock market.

48

What prompts the Federal Reserve Board to raise or lower interest rates? Are there any indicators that can help individual investors like me anticipate the moves of the Fed?

Fears or concerns about the economy prompt the Federal Reserve to adjust interest rates. (Fear of inflation can cause the Fed to raise interest rates, and fear of recession or economic slowdown prompts the Fed to lower interest rates.) Some of the indicators you may wish to keep an eye on are:

- ◆ **Producer Price Index (PPI).** An excellent indicator of future price increases or decreases.
- ◆ **Consumer Price Indexes (CPI).** A survey of housing prices, utilities, consumer products and services.
- ◆ **Gross Domestic Product.** Measures growth or business activity. (Generally, when GDP is above 3%, it is considered inflationary.)
- ◆ **Capacity Utilization.** A measurement of the rate in which plants and utilities operate as a percent of total capacity.
- ◆ **Employment and Unemployment Data.** As employment figures go up, more employment creates more demand for workers. This results in higher wages, which are considered inflationary.

49

When the Dow Jones average goes up or down 50 points, I noticed CNBC prints *NYSE curbs* on the side of the screen. What does this mean? Also, what does the *NYSE Circuit Breaker* mean?

The New York Stock Exchange shuts down trading for 30 minutes when the Dow Jones Industrial Average (DJIA) drops 350 points in one day. The move is intended to cool off traders and investors and is called a *circuit breaker*. If the DJIA drops another 200 points that same day, NYSE stops trading for another hour.

The NYSE has a curb on computer-aided trading when the DJIA goes up or down 50 points in one day. When this occurs, CNBC tells viewers by noting *NYSE curbs"* on the screen.

50

What is the "retirement gender gap?"

Very simply, women outlive men, and need their retirement assets to sustain them for six years longer. That's the *retirement gender gap*. According to KPMG Peat Marwick, women over age 25 are employed an average of 4.8 years for every 6.6 years that men work. Frequently, full vesting in corporate pension plans requires five years of continuous employment. Since women tend to earn 63% of the salary of a male colleague, and receive fewer pension benefits, they will be forced to save a greater portion of their incomes in order to have the same standard of living as men do when they retire.

51

I've heard it mentioned that women need to earn higher returns on their investments than men. Why?

Some analysts say that, because women tend to earn only 63% of what men make, they have to catch up by making sure they earn higher returns on their investments. This may be valid in many situations, and I do not dispute their answer. However, even if we assume that there is no difference in pay between genders, women still need to earn a higher return simply because they usually live about six years longer than men usually do.

According to the National Council for Health Statistics, among Americans born in 1950 who attain age 65, men are projected to live to age 81 while women are projected to live to age 87. This means that because many women often care for the children, they spend fewer years in the work force and enjoy fewer pension benefits.

52

I am a retired businessman and my wife has no interest in understanding our investments. Any suggestions for arranging our finances so that my wife will receive a steady monthly income if I become incapacitated or die before her?

It sounds as if you want your investments to run on automatic pilot so that your wife does not have to make any decisions or changes. You can create a portfolio of quality diversified mutual funds and arrange for your wife to receive a systematic monthly withdrawal. The total of each year's withdrawals should be 6-8% of your original investment.

In addition, if you and your financial advisor pick the right blend of stock funds, plus, for some people, balanced mutual funds, your nest egg will be protected against inflation.

Balanced funds may be useful because, historically, they have returned 10-11% a year during the past 30 years. If that historic return continues, even if your wife's withdrawals total 8% a year, your balanced funds will still make money.

Balanced funds, incidentally, usually buy a mixture of common and preferred stock, plus bonds. The idea here is to get income plus enough growth to protect your nest egg from being cracked by inflation.

53

My company downsized me after 17 years of loyal service. Any suggestions for me?

I've been there. I was working for a Fortune 500 company that eliminated my job, and I was crushed. My wife was three months pregnant with our first child at the time.

That was a number of years ago. Now, when I conduct financial seminars for out placement firms, I tell people about that experience. I tell people that the only out placement my employer gave me was to say "clean out your desk by five o'clock today."

To get another job, you have to understand the ins and outs of the hiring process. The easiest and quickest way of doing that is to visit either your local bookstore or the main branch of your library. Get five or ten books on the subject. Study them so that you understand what the process is like and what you need to do. Remember, unlike the stock market, the job market is very fragmented and often difficult to find. To uncover 80% of all jobs, you must spend 80% of your time networking. The other 20% of your time — but only 20% — you can give to answering newspaper ads, conducting mailings, and visiting employment agencies and executive recruiters.

What is networking? Letting people know you're looking for a job and what kind of job you're looking for. Contact all your friends, acquaintances, associates, former employers, and suppliers, plus people in the same civic, social and alumni groups as you're in.

Job hunting itself is a fulltime job. And it's lonely. You have to motivate and discipline yourself. Nobody else can. You can't wait for others to call you; you must call first. Your spirits almost certainly will sag at some point during your job search, especially when you know you're doing everything right and your savings are sinking lower and lower.

Your family and friends may also feel frustrated. They want to help, but are powerless to wave a magic wand and make a good job offer appear for you.

Before you go to a job interview, *prepare, prepare, prepare.* Learn as much as you can about the company. Get information from the library, trade journals, local newspaper, and former employees, as well as suppliers and customers. If you do prepare, you'll walk into that interview knowing the company's size and profitability, plus its strengths and weaknesses. You'll also know its reputation among suppliers, customers, and competitors.

The interviewer will be impressed with how much you know and probably will conclude that you understand the company and its business. You want to make that kind of impression.

When I was unemployed, it was hard for me to believe that my parents were right when they told me everything works out for the best. In my case, it did. I sincerely hope you will be able to say the same after your search is through.

54

I'm a recent widow. My husband managed all of our investments for more than fifty years — while I raised our children. I am afraid to manage these investments because I have no experience in financial planning. I can't afford to lose this money. But I also don't want to have to depend upon a stranger for my financial well-being. What should I do?

Many women are in your situation because many women have, historically, married men five to ten years older than themselves. Also, women outlive men by six years on the average. This means that many women are widows for fifteen to twenty years. Many women who are currently in their sixties or seventies never worked outside of their homes. They raised their children while their husbands earned a living and managed the family's investments. They had no preparation, knowledge or experience of financial matters because their husbands took care of everything. Unfortunately, they have no choice now that they are widows. They must assume responsibility because no one else will. *You must recognize that no one is more concerned about your money than you are.*

You can start to become knowledgeable by attending seminars, reading some basic books on investment, or enrolling in a local adult education course. And don't be afraid to ask questions. If you have a relationship with a broker or financial consultant, insist that this person explains everything that you feel you should know about. If you are uncomfortable with anything about an investment, make sure it's clarified to your satisfaction. If you have a broker who wants to take over and asks you to sign a discretionary account, be aware that you are giving that person limited control over your finances.

By having some basic knowledge about investing, you will be able to ask the right questions. You'll feel confident that you are making good decisions about your own well-being, and are not dependent upon others for your financial health.

Let me stress once more the importance of not being afraid to ask a question about your portfolio because you feel "it's a dumb question." The only dumb question is the one you were too embarrassed to ask. Remember, it is your money, so go ahead and ask that question!

55

My son is a sophomore in college. Recently he asked me which career would provide the best job security. What should I tell him?

Tell him that job security is an oxymoron. It is an anachronism not only in America, but also in almost all modern societies. Even U.S. Military and U.S. Naval Academy career officers who were combat veterans in the Persian Gulf are being separated from the service prior to retirement.

The concept of working for one company for 30-40 years and then retiring is outdated. Companies that were known for never laying off employees (like IBM) are using all sorts of euphemisms to verbally soften the impact of firing employees for economic reasons. "Downsizing," "outplacing," "de-jobbing," and "discharging" are some of the terms used.

The dwindling size of Fortune 500 Corporation work forces has motivated many displaced employees to operate small businesses out of their homes. These small businesses are frequently linked electronically (by fax, e-mail, and Internet) which enables these entrepreneurs to benefit from flexible working time and more creative environments. They have been the fuel that's fed our economy's most recent recovery.

What can your son do to prepare himself so that he has

job security when he graduates? He must realize that he really is in business for himself, and needs to market himself on a temporary basis to his employer, knowing that his position is temporary. Realizing this temporary state of employment, he must be constantly improving his marketable skills and must always be ready to adapt to changes in the workplace.

Tell your son that he needs to develop public speaking skills, become computer proficient and (especially if he wishes to go into business in an internationally diverse region like California, Arizona, Texas or Florida) be able to speak and understand Spanish. He can learn public speaking at schools or at Toastmasters clubs. Why Spanish? Within 4-5 years, approximately 20% of the U.S. population will speak Spanish as a primary language. Spanish speakers represent one of the fastest growing segments of our population.

56

What will happen when baby boomers begin to retire?

It is estimated that in 2010, when baby boomers start to reach age 65, the number of retirees will soar. During the next decade, the overall population growth in the U.S. is expected to grow at approximately 2% while population growth for retirees is expected to exceed 25%. Currently, about 3.3 working Americans support one retiree. When the baby boomers begin to retire in 2011, it is estimated that three working Americans will support *one* retiree.

Reducing Social Security or Medicare benefits is a hot potato that almost all politicians refuse to touch because they fear that retirees in their districts will vote them out of office at the next election if they do take a position.

The more politically palatable remedy will be to increase the age when retirement benefits begin. Complicating this formula are unknowns such as increasing longevity due to medical advances like genetic engineering and discoveries of cures for diseases (especially those affecting the elderly).

If the aging process can be delayed by medical advances and discoveries (as some foresee), the retirement age in 25-40 years may be 75-80 years.

57

How does the stock market perform during pre-election years?

Since 1940, pre-election years have been by far the best-performing years for the market. Realizing that past performance is no indication of future results, the numbers for the past 50+ years for the S&P index with dividends reinvested are:

Pre-election year average	+21.05%
Election year average	+12.40%
Post-election year average	+ 7.81%
Mid-term election year average	+10.23%

58

What is the NASD?

NASD stands for the National Association of Securities Dealers. The NASD operates under the supervision of the Securities and Exchange Commission (SEC), and under fair and equitable rules of securities trading.

59

What is the NASDAQ?

NASDAQ stands for *National Association of Securities Dealers Automated Quotation System.* It is the "over-the-counter" market and usually lists stocks of smaller companies. NASDAQ is owned and operated by the National Association Securities Dealers (NASD) and is a computerized system providing pricing information.

60

How does indexing work?

Indexing is a way to remove the effects of inflation when calculating benefits for special groups, or when measuring real results from an investment. For example, benefits for both Social Security recipients and military retirees are indexed to the Consumer Price Index (CPI).

By using indexing to compute the real rate of return, some tax reformers suggest that home owners will not be penalized when selling homes that have appreciated solely because of inflation. Others recommend that indexing be used to calculate capital gains for all investments.

61

What is a flat tax?

A flat tax was widely discussed during the 1996 Presidential campaign. The leading voice in that movement was Steve Forbes, publisher of *Forbes* Magazine and a Republican presidential nomination candidate. Under his plan, all income would be taxed at one rate with no deductions.

62

What would happen if a flat tax was passed?

The tax code would be very simple. Mortgage interest and property tax deductions would no longer be allowed and the real estate market probably would be affected. Charitable donations would no longer be tax deductible. Retirement account 401ks, IRAs, Keoghs, would no longer be tax deferred. Medical, hospital expenses would not be deductible.

There would be considerable pain in the IRS and accounting firms because they would employ far fewer people. The 1996 electorate did not seem to take the flat tax seriously and Forbes' candidacy was short-lived.

63

What would happen to tax-free bonds under a flat tax?

Tax-free bonds issued by cities, counties and states would no longer be tax-free. The interest on those bonds would be taxable, just as Treasuries are now. Because the U.S. government has better credit rating than the states, cities and counties, municipal bonds would have to yield more than Treasuries. Currently, tax-free municipal bonds yield approximately 80% of the yield on a 30-year Treasury bond.

64

What is the relationship between the budget deficit, the national debt, and the stock market?

The *budget deficit* (which is computed annually) is the difference between the amount of receipts and expenditures of our federal budget. (By the way, the sum of the annual budget deficits since this country was founded equals the total national debt of our nation today.)

As the debt service (interest payments to bond holders) of our *national debt* increases (representing a bigger drain on our economy), the *stock market* suffers. Currently, one of six dollars raised in taxes is used to pay interest on our national debt. As this debt increases, we will have less money to pay for capital investment and to rebuild the infrastructure of our country. That threatens to reduce our standard of living, and will certainly depress the stock market.

65

Isn't most of the U.S. national debt in the hands of foreigners?

No. Approximately $1.2 trillion worth of U.S. Treasury bonds are in the hands of foreigners. This figure seems immense, and it is. But it is only 22% of the national debt, which is currently about $5.4 trillion. The largest holders of the national debt are domestic pension funds.

66

What are the entitlements causing the federal budget deficit to rise?

The federal budget deficit is the difference between how much money the government takes in and how much it pays out. For many years, the federal government has been spending more than it has been getting. However, the annual budget deficit has been going down since 1992.

Social entitlement programs pay benefits to all people in a specific category who are entitled to them. That's why they're called entitlement programs. Three of the top five federal expenditures include entitlement programs. According to recent Treasury Department figures, the top five expenditures are: Social Security (23%), defense (16%), national debt interest (15%), Medicare (12%) and Medicaid (6%).

67

Do you think Social Security will be around when I am ready to retire? I am 29 years old.

A recent survey asked Americans in their 20s — your age group — about their attitude and opinion of Social Security. More of them believed in the existence of UFOs than that they would someday receive Social Security benefits. Social Security will survive — but benefits will probably decrease as older eligibility ages are established. The normal retirement age of 65 years will begin to change in the year 2000. This will affect those born after 1937 and the eligibility age will gradually increase to 67.

You must take responsibility for your retirement by realizing Social Security will provide only a base level of income during your retirement years. It was never intended to function as a retirement plan but only as a supplement. You need to shoulder your retirement needs by starting to invest in tax-deferred investments such as IRAs, 401(k) plans, SEPs, and Keoghs when you are young so that time and compound interest will make your retirement nest egg multiply. Never before has a comfortable retirement depended more on personal financial planning and disciplined savings.

68

Are my Social Security contributions deposited into a separate Social Security Trust Fund which grows as my taxes are added to it?

No, they're not. There is no separate Social Security Trust Fund. That fact involves some political and budgetary hocus-pocus which lets politicians claim the federal budget is more balanced than it really is. *Newsweek* magazine has called this maneuver "budget flimflam."

Here's what really happens to your Social Security contributions: The federal government takes the money you and your employer have paid into your Social Security account. Then, instead of earmarking that money specifically for Social Security benefits, the government deposits it into the same pot with the federal income taxes the IRS collects every year. That pot is called General Revenue.

The amount you contribute to Social Security every year is more than the government pays out in Social Security benefits. That excess, currently about $80 billion a year is not used to beef up the Social Security fund for future recipients. Instead, that surplus is used to offset the federal deficit. That accounting maneuver is allowed because social security contributions are in the General Revenue pot and not put into a separate, earmarked category.

This problem is growing worse. The Congressional Budget Office estimates that by the year 2001, Social Security payroll taxes will be used to offset nearly $100 billion of the federal deficit.

69

I've heard the term "sandwich generation." What does it mean?

The "sandwich generation" refers to the generation (usually in their 40s or 50s now), who are supporting elderly parents as well as providing financial support for their children (usually by paying for their college educations). This generation is *sandwiched* between an older and younger generation.

In addition to be sandwiched between parents and their children, many are trying to provide for their own retirements. They may also be faced with the possibility of downsizing within their own companies and are concerned about the possible loss of their livelihoods. All this pressure to balance conflicting demands creates considerable stress. To compound this problem, their adult children may be part of the "baby boomerang" generation. (These are adult children who have left the family nest and later return to live with their parents.)

70

I am sandwiched between the responsibilities of saving for my child's college costs, supporting a disabled elderly parent and contributing to my 401(k) plan at work. I have limited financial resources and I feel torn between conflicting demands. What should I do?

Your situation is becoming increasingly common among baby-boomers. You must decide what you feel most comfortable doing, then live with those decisions.

Because your child's eligibility for college aid is reduced by any money in his or her name. I suggest you forgo saving for your child's college costs and provide for your parent instead. Also, if you are in the 31% tax bracket, every $1,000 you contribute to your 401k Plan will reduce your income taxes by $310.

71

Would you explain the difference between growth stocks and income stocks?

Growth stocks, as their name suggests, offer above-average growth that exceeds the rate of inflation. If you are seeking to benefit from your investments in five years or more and don't need current income, you'll probably benefit more by investing in growth stocks, especially if they are in a tax-sheltered retirement account such as IRA or 401(k) plan.

Income stocks provide relatively high-paying dividends; utilities used to be in this category until 1993-1994. There is a trade off between income and growth. Many retirees in their 60s mistakenly seek to maximize their current returns or current incomes by forsaking growth in their portfolios. These retirees are positioning themselves to be victimized by inflation if they live a normal or longer-than-normal life span.

72

How can I learn more about investing so that I don't have to depend upon others for my financial well-being?

Attend more seminars, enroll in a basic adult education course in your community, get an overview by reading some of the "How to" books in this store or from your local library.

73

Can you recommend any books on investing?

Making The Most Of Your Money by Jane Bryant Quinn is an easy-to-follow step-by-step guide about organizing your financial affairs. Ms. Quinn is a columnist for *Newsweek* magazine and is syndicated in 250 newspapers nationwide.

There are many other excellent books on investing, such as Peter Lynch's *Beating The Street*. He writes in an easy-to-understand manner, avoids jargon and makes sense. Mr. Lynch earned his reputation as a manager of the Fidelity Magellan Fund.

Another book is *Stocks for the Long Run: A Guide For Selecting Markets for Long-Term Growth* by Jeremy Siegel, professor of finance at the Wharton School, University of Pennsylvania. The book makes a strong case for investing in stocks rather than bonds over the long run, by showing that a 40-year-old saving for retirement can expect much higher returns from stocks than bonds. Dr. Siegel was recently voted *Best Business School Professor* by *Business Week* magazine.

The Great Boom Ahead by Harry S. Dent, Jr. is an upbeat forecast for investors on the reasons they will prosper during America's protracted boom. After reading this book I felt very positive about our economy. Dent believes that as the baby boomers reach their peak spending years (ages 45-50), this spending wave will result in a Great Boom. Dent presents a very persuasive case for investing in equities to capitalize on *The Great Boom Ahead.*

Independently Wealthy by Robert Goodman offers a roadmap anyone can follow to build financial security.

In addition to reading these books, you may wish to enroll in an adult education course at your local high school or college.

74

Can you recommend some magazines I can read to be better informed about my investments?

A lot depends upon your background, education, investment experience, available time and financial situation. Some of the magazines to which I subscribe are *Forbes, Fortune, The Economist, Florida Trend, Consumer Reports, US News & World Report, Barron's, South Florida Business Journal, Business in Broward* magazine, *Wharton, Newsweek* and *Bottom Line* newsletter. In addition, I read two local newspapers and *The Wall Street Journal* each morning. At my office, there are company publications that help keep me informed about the markets. I confess that I am frequently frustrated because I don't have enough time to read all of them.

If you're just starting out and have no prior investment experience or knowledge, *Kiplinger's Personal Finance* magazine is an excellent choice. I suggest you attend seminars that are not pushing a specific product, and try watching CNN Financial News or CNBC channels on cable television or the *Nightly Business Report* on public broadcasting television stations.

Chapter 4

Retirement

In the last decade, we have been forced to assume more and more responsibility for our comfortable retirement. That's because today's employers have increasingly switched from retirement plans with defined benefits to defined contribution retirement plans. Most of these plans are different than government pensions — they lack cost-of-living adjustments (COLAS). Under these plans, you — not your employer — are solely responsible for ensuring that your investments will adequately fund your retirement.

With the average retirement now spanning 20 to 30 years, the major concern for most investors is the danger of outliving one's assets. Taxes have increased and investors are concerned about reduced earnings on their future incomes. Increased taxes have affected social security recipients; 85% of social security benefits are taxed for retirees with joint incomes of $44,000 or more and individual incomes of $34,000 or more.

The most-asked questions at my seminars at libraries and

book stores are from retirees and pre-retirees. Many are exasperated by the effects of inflation but are too risk-averse to put a major part of their portfolios in investments that normally grow faster than the inflation rate. Playing it too safe by investing in CDs is threatening their purchasing power.

Many brochures printed by banks, mutual fund companies and brokerage firms are entitled "How Can I Afford Retirement?" or "Are You Prepared To Live To Age 85, 90 or 95?" "Are You Saving Enough Or Investing Enough For Retirement?" "Will You Be Able To Afford To Send Your Children To The College Of Their Choice?" One recent ad by a major brokerage firm caught my attention with its dramatic message. "Imagine the cost of putting 15 kids through an Ivy League college and you'll have some idea of what you'll need for a comfortable retirement."

By taking advantage of 401(k) and other employee-sponsored plans, you reduce your taxable income by the amount you invest via payroll deductions. If you are self-employed, take advantage of the benefits of establishing a qualified retirement plan such as an Individual Retirement Account (IRA), Simplified Employee Plan (SEP) or a Keogh Plan.

75

What can I do to make sure I don't outlive my retirement assets?

This is the number one concern for most investors. People are living longer and longer, and they're right to be concerned that they might outlive their savings.

To put the problem in a nutshell, if you can ensure that your retirement assets grow faster than the rate of inflation, then you will never outlive your retirement assets.

One way to ensure that you will not outlive your retirement assets is to have long-term health care insurance, so that your assets are not depleted in order to provide living expenses in case you're ill or incapacitated. You need to get this insurance while you are healthy and insurable.

76

What is the cost of procrastinating in beginning an investment plan?

Many people intend to contribute to their retirement plans or establish a college education for their infant son or daughter — but fail to follow through.

The price of this procrastination can be staggering. The chart below shows the difference in growth between an individual who makes a one-time $10,000 contribution to a retirement plan at age 25 and an individual who makes that $10,000 contribution 10 years later, at age 35. (This assumes the $10,000 is invested in a tax sheltered investment with an annual rate of 10%.) In addition, the benefits of compounding are severely reduced by procrastinating.

The cost of waiting to invest $10,000:

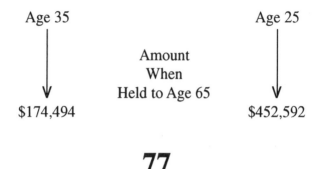

Age 35	Amount When Held to Age 65	Age 25
$174,494		$452,592

77

I am 48 years old, self-employed, recently divorced and have been unable to start saving for retirement. Is it too late to start a retirement program?

It's never too late. Many people have been interrupted in their retirement planning by a divorce or the loss of a job. Start saving now. If you look at the alternative, you can't afford *not* to start saving for your retirement.

78

What would happen to my IRA (Individual Retirement Account) if I die before I cash it in? What about taxes?

After your death, your beneficiary will have several choices for receiving the proceeds from your IRA. The 10% penalty tax doesn't apply to these distributions, regardless of your age or your beneficiary's age. However, the distribution is subject, however, to income taxes (except for amounts that represent a return of nondeductible contributions). Thus, how your beneficiary elects to receive the proceeds can have a significant effect on the tax bill.

For example, if you had already started taking the required distributions because you were over age 70-1/2, your beneficiary could continue to take periodic distributions on the same schedule. If your distributions had not yet begun, the relationship of the beneficiary to the owner will determine how the funds may be withdrawn.

Surviving spouses have the most options. Your spouse can cash in all or part of the IRA without paying the 10% penalty. Or your spouse can roll over the IRA to his/her own IRA, making the money subject to the same rules as his/her own IRA. (Thus he or she would pay a 10% penalty tax if the funds were withdrawn before the age of 59-1/2 and withdrawals must start by age 70-1/2.) Another option is to allow the funds to remain in your IRA. The funds can remain in your IRA until the year you would have turned 70-1/2, at which time your spouse would have to start taking distributions based upon his or her life expectancy.

If your beneficiary is not your spouse, he or she has two basic options. Either funds can be withdrawn from the IRA within five years, or the beneficiary can start to take withdrawals within one year of your death (based upon his or her life expectancy). It is important that you name a beneficiary for your IRA in order to make these options available to your heirs. If you don't have a beneficiary and someone inherits your IRA under a will, their only option is to cash in the entire balance in the IRA within five years.

79

What is a SEP Retirement Plan? Does it require a lot of paperwork to open?

SEP stands for *Simplified Employee Pension Plan* (it is sometimes referred to as a SEP-IRA). A SEP is an employer-sponsored retirement savings program; the paperwork required to open one consists only of a one-page agreement.

SEPs are much less complicated to establish and maintain than traditional pension plans are, and they offer more benefits than a standard IRA. A standard IRA only allows annual tax-deductible contributions of up to $2,000, whereas a SEP permits contributions up to 15% of annual compensation (up to $24,000).

Contributions to a SEP are a tax-deductible expense. Even if you are in a one-man or one-woman business, you're eligible for a SEP.

80

I work for a Fortune 500 company and have enrolled in its 401(k) retirement plan. There are about a half dozen investments for me to choose from. What should I do?

A lot depends upon your investment objectives and your age. If you have five or more years until retirement, you may wish to look for growth. Don't keep most of your money in money market funds, government obligation or bond funds. Rather, invest your money in growth funds (both domestic and international). This will keep you ahead of inflation.

Since there are more than 8,000 mutual funds available on the market today, it is very hard to recommend funds without knowing first which funds are offered on your 401(k) selection menu. If you have a financial consultant, let him or her know about your 401(k) plan and ask for recommendations. Even though your consultant does not directly benefit from your 401(k) plan, I believe that he or she will probably extend the courtesy of helping you since you give him other business.

81

Am I better off investing my IRA in a Standard & Poor 500 index fund, considering that these funds do better than 90% of the mutual funds?

No. Avoid the putting-all-your-eggs-in-one-basket trap. The S&P 500 includes only one sector: large companies. If you invested in such a fund during the 1990s, you've done well. But if you bought that same index fund in 1962 and held it until 1974, your portfolio wouldn't have grown one inch.

82

As a retiree, how can I maintain my current income (while interest rates are declining) without increasing my risk?

This depends upon what your current investments are. If your current investments are CDs and money market funds, and you wish to increase your return, you will have to increase your risk. There is a strong relationship between risk and reward. You can't avoid some risk of principal if you try to increase your return. However, if you have no risk of principal and your return is less than the rate of inflation, you will lose money each year.

83

We have a 401(k) plan at work and I haven't participated because I just don't understand it. It seems so complicated. Would you explain what a 401(k) plan is and how it works in simple terms so that I can understand it?

A 401(k) plan is a voluntary retirement program sponsored by your employer. It provides you with an opportunity to save for your retirement through payroll deductions, which are made before taxes are withheld. In addition to deferring taxes on the amount of your contributions, the earnings on these amounts will compound even faster than they would otherwise because all taxes are deferred until you start withdrawing them from your 401(k) retirement plan.

Some companies match employee contributions up to a certain amount or percentage. This is an excellent opportunity to double your money instantly. According to *Kiplinger's Personal Finance* magazine, approximately 25% of eligible employees do not participate in their companies' 401(k) plans.

84

Is borrowing from a 401(k) plan a good strategy?

No. If you are no longer employed, you may be required to pay back the money your 401(k) loaned you. If you can't pay if back and are under 59^1/$_2$, you will pay a 10% penalty on it PLUS regular income taxes.

You'll lose even more money than that. Whatever money you borrowed stops compounding. That's money for your 20-30 year retirement you will not have and will never see.

85

If I withdraw funds from my retirement plan, what are the tax consequences?

If you are under age 59$\frac{1}{2}$, there is a 10% penalty on the amount withdrew plus regular income tax on the amount withdrawn. In addition to the tax consequences, premature withdrawals from investments earmarked to provide for your retirement deny you the benefits of compounding — and of feeling financially secure about your future.

86

What happens to my 401(k) retirement plan if I change jobs?

If you wish, you can leave your 401(k) retirement plan in place at your former employer or you can roll over your retirement plan into an IRA rollover plan. In order to avoid a tax consequence, it is essential for you to roll over your 401(k) plan directly to an IRA rollover at a brokerage firm or bank. If you take a distribution, twenty percent will be withheld for taxes.

87

Is there an excess tax if I take out more than a certain amount from IRA?

Yes. Starting in 1987, the IRS started levying a 15% excise tax on excess IRA distributions or payouts, higher than $155,000. The Business Job Protection Act of 1996 suspended this tax for 1997, 1998 and 1999. For these years, all distributions are taxed at the rate you ordinarily pay. However IRA distributions you receive before age 59$\frac{1}{2}$ have an additional 10% penalty.

88

Next year I plan to retire. Should I start to withdraw money from my IRA or my investment account to support myself?

Since your taxable investments will grow slower than your IRA, cash in your taxable investments first. As your IRA grows, its earnings are not taxed as long as they are not touched. This is the reason tax-deferred investments such as an IRA generally grow faster than your investment account.

All of us will need to maximize the growth of our retirement portfolios as our life expectancies and cost of living rises. Never before have retirees been as challenged to assume personal responsibility if they wish to enjoy a comfortable lifestyle for 20-30 years.

89

I am enrolled in a 401k plan at work and have selected to invest in my company's common stock because it has been the best performing choice. What do you think?

It's a risky business. About 40% of all 401(k) participants invest exclusively in their own company out of loyalty or obligation. In addition, companies frequently match employee 401(k) contributions partially or entirely with company stock. The danger: If you have all your money in one stock, you lose big if that stock goes down.

Instead, diversify, diversify, diversify. Shrink your 401(k) risk by spreading your money into several mutual funds. If you have a good relationship with your investment advisor, ask his or her opinion of your choices. I help many clients with their 401(k) plans even though I don't get paid for doing it.

90

Can I open an IRA (Individual Retirement Account) for my infant daughter?

Yes, you can open an IRA for your daughter — if she earns income. For instance, if she earns income as a child model or actress, that would be considered earned income. The amount of her earned income (up to $2,000) could be used to open an IRA, and the portion up to $2,000 would be deducted from her taxable income taxes.

    Because of the benefits of compounding, opening an IRA account for children who have earned income is an excellent idea. For example, let's look at a grandparent with a grandchild who earned $2,000. If this IRA were opened when the child was 14, and every year $ 2,000 was contributed to this IRA for the next six years, the total contributions would be $12,000. Through compounding, and earning a 10% return annually, the earnings would grow tax-deferred. When that grandchild becomes 65 years old, he or she will have earned more than $1 million.

91

I am 38 years old. Seven years ago, I moved to France from Chicago so I could own and operate an Italian restaurant. When I quit my Chicago job, I left the money in my retirement plan with that employer. Now that I live abroad, is there any way to get that money without paying taxes on it?

No. You can postpone taxes on your retirement plan, but there's no way to eliminate them. The law lets you avoid paying taxes on the income you contributed to your retirement plan. In addition, the money your investments earn in that plan are not taxed either. But money in your plan is protected from taxes only until you pull it out.

In your case, any withdrawals now would be taxed. The money you take out of that plan, no matter what your age, is subject to ordinary income taxes. To make your situation worse, you are below age 59$^1/_2$. Any money you take out of your retirement plan before that age is considered premature. That means you'll get socked with an additional 10% penalty.

92

What do you think of senior lifecare centers for retirees?

Today's senior citizens are very different from their parents. Technological, medical, and social changes occurring during the past generation have modified the lives and expectations of senior citizens in the 1990s. When many of us were growing up, it was common to have one's grandmother living with the family. As grandmothers became widows and grandfathers became widowers, they moved in to their children's homes. This was the norm.

During the past 20-30 years, more families have become two-working-parent households. Both parents struggle to keep up with the increasing costs of living, the uncertainties caused by down-sizing or lack of job security, and galloping cost of medical services and college tuitions. These people are less able to take care of their elderly parents than prior generations were. Coupled with this dilemma, people are living much longer these days. The major concerns of today's seniors are:

◆ Maintaining their independence and not being a burden to children or spouse.
◆ Outliving their savings.
◆ Not being able to sustain their standard of living as they become older.
◆ Not being able to drive, maintain their home, or feel safe and secure in their home.

Today's economic realities have created a need for lifecare centers for senior citizens to live in while they are healthy. These are not nursing homes designed for those unable to care for themselves, but are adult communities that provides complete freedom for its residents. The arrangement seems to satisfy a need for companionship. The responsibilities and hassles of home-ownership are eliminated.

Since many retirees relocate to warmer climates, their children may be more than 1,000 miles away. These communities provide a way to be independent for those having the financial means and good health.

93

What should I look for when checking out the facilities of adult communities?

If you know people who are living at a community you're considering, you have an excellent source of information. Visit at different times of the day and week, talk to the residents, and ask what they like. Ask them if they had to do it over again would they select this community? If there was anything they would like to change, what would it be?

◆ Find out what happens when and if health problems occur. What facilities are available? What are the costs?

◆ Learn about annual fees and the rate of increases for these fees.

◆ Find out what transportation facilities are available when residents can no longer drive their cars.

◆ Examine the financial statements of the community. What kind of reputation does it have? Is it a public company? If so, have your financial consultant get a 10(k) report and annual report to analyze.

◆ If possible, include your children and/or grandchildren in the decision-making process. Their input may be invaluable because they may see or ask about areas that you have overlooked.

The more information you have, the more comfortable you will probably feel making a decision. Many senior citizens, when visiting a community for the first time, say, "This is a great idea, but I'm just not ready." Once they make their move, though, they often say, "I wish I had done this sooner."

Senior communities provide people with adult companionship and help eliminate anxiety about being victimized by crime or being alone when one becomes injured or ill. As baby boomers enter their 60s, these living arrangements will probably grow in popularity.

94

Why is it that some people do not purchase long term care insurance?

Many people believe that Medicare will cover their nursing home costs. The fact is Medicare pays less than 3% of these costs. It was established to provide for short-term medical attention and not intended to be used for basic care such as bathing and dressing. In rare cases that Medicare covers skilled care costs it pays only up to 100 days. In the United States, the average stay in a nursing home exceeds 450 days.

Some people think they will qualify for Medicaid coverage if they transfer their assets to family members and thereby become reduced to a state of poverty. But Medicaid has strict regulations against transferring assets to others in order to qualify for Medicaid benefits. In addition, many people would prefer not to see their life savings wasted to pay their nursing home bills.

Others do not want to face the prospect of needing long term care insurance and deny this possibility by saying "it won't happen to me." It is estimated that approximately 50% of all Americans aged 65 and over can expect to reside in a nursing home at one time or another.

95

Do I need Medigap insurance?

It's certainly advisable. Medigap insurance covers part or all of your medical expenses Medicare doesn't pay. Your annual premium, of course, depends on the benefits you pick. I recommend buying Medigap insurance within 6 months after you join Medicare.

96

Why should I buy comprehensive long-term care insurance when I can buy home health care coverage for about half of the cost? I've visited nursing homes and I never want to live in one. My wife can take care of me.

Don't count on it. Being old and sick is troubling. Being old, sick and not getting the care you need can be frightening.

Long term care insurance covers custodial care costs Medicare doesn't pay. It pays whether your care is at home or in a nursing home. Home-health care insurance only pays for your primary care giver to have assistance at home.

In your case, the primary care-giver would be your wife — only if she is healthy enough and outlives you. Have you figured out who will take care of you if she is no longer alive or too ill? For that matter, who is going to take care of her if you can't?

If you are sick and your wife can't be there for you, the yearly cost of 24-hour professional health care at home may top $200,000. The premium for home health care coverage which would pay that expense costs more than most people can afford if it were available.

This situation is a lot more likely than you think. Many people being cared for at home gradually deteriorate to a point where they must have 24-hour professional care. If your home health care coverage does not pay that entire expense, you or your wife must. Furthermore, 24-hour care is more readily available in a nursing home. If you only have home health care coverage, your coverage stops at the nursing home door.

97

How can I make sure that I get all of the Social Security benefits to which I'm entitled when I retire in four years?

You can request a statement listing your estimated benefits and total annual earnings. Request a *Personal Earnings and Benefits Estimate* (PEBES) form by calling 1-800-772-1213. The Social Security Administration will send it to you within one week.

98

Should I start drawing reduced Social Security benefits at age 62 or wait until age 65 to receive full benefits?

If you start receiving social security benefits at age 62, your monthly check will be 80% of what it would have been if you would have waited until you reached age 65. You are penalized $5/9$ of 1%, or a factor of 0.005555 for every month you start Social Security before age 62. Then the 36 months you have cashed in early will be used to figure out your penalty. For example, if you were going to receive a monthly Social Security check of $1000 by waiting until age 65, but you started at age 62, here's how the government would calculate your monthly penalty:

36 months x $1,000 x 0.00555 = $199.98 penalty;
$1000 - 199.98 = 800.02 early retirement monthly check.

You should know that you'll have to reach age 77 before the total amount you receive by waiting until age 65 will be more than what you'd get if you started at age 62. Other factors you may want to consider include whether you need the money at age 62, and the effects of inflation, neither of which are considered here.

99

What do you suggest that I do with my 401(k) plan distribution if my job is eliminated through downsizing?

You have four options:
- ◆ No change. Keep your monies invested in your existing 401(k) plan if your employer's plan allows it. Your investment choices are very limited within most 401(k) plans.
- ◆ Direct rollover. Your distribution is directly rollovered into an IRA or another qualified plan.
- ◆ Indirect rollover. Your funds are paid directly to you after 20% is withheld.
- ◆ Cash in your account. By receiving a distribution, you'll have to pay taxes and possible penalties.

The best option, number 2, is to retain tax-deferred status of your retirement plan by opening an IRA direct rollover account.

Number 3, the indirect rollover, when you take personal receipt of your 401(k) plan distribution and arrange to deposit these funds into your IRA. (If you choose to receive the funds directly, your former employer is required to withhold 20% for federal income tax.) You then may roll over the remaining funds (80%) into your IRA. You are required to roll over these funds within 60 days of receipt. When you file your income tax return, you then file for a refund of the 20% of your distribution withheld.

By electing the second option (a direct rollover), you will avoid the mandatory 20% withholding and have your total lump sum distribution fully invested. Approximately 70% of individuals eligible to receive a lump sum distribution because of a change or loss of jobs elect to receive these funds. This is the fourth option.

The amount received is considered income and taxed accordingly. If you are younger than $59\frac{1}{2}$ when you receive this distribution, there is an additional a 10% penalty.

Chapter 5

Understanding Equities

Investments in common stocks have proven to be the best long-term protection against inflation. Numerous convincing studies have concluded that proper asset allocation is responsible for more than 90% of the return for individual portfolios. Asset allocation is the process of determining which classes of assets to invest in. Dividend reinvestment plans are an excellent way to improve returns.

Many investors are apprehensive about the ups and downs of the stock market and want a "safer, less-risky investment." They believe the safest investments for them, as conservative investors, are insured bank accounts, CDs, and United States Treasury bills. But the fact is this: These investments are not designed for growth or inflation protection; they are secure only in that you will be guaranteed return of your principal.

Stocks usually perform better than bonds over the long run even though their values tend to fluctuate more over the course of any given week or month or year. There are various types of stocks designed to meet the needs of all investors: conservative, moderate and aggressive.

◆ **Blue-chip stocks** comprise large, well-established corporations that have more predictable earnings. Ironically, these are companies that have been reducing their work forces to try to become more globally competitive.

◆ **Growth stocks** are more volatile than blue-chips, but offer higher potential for appreciation.

◆ **Small company stocks** have the greatest risks and potential for appreciation.

You can reduce your risk by:

◆ diversifying among several classes of stocks.

◆ proper asset allocation.

◆ staying invested over the long run in spite of temporary down markets.

◆ be diversified in your employer sponsored 403(b) or 401(k) plan.

Value Line and Morningstar are rating services that, respectively, publish comprehensive one-page reports on common stocks and mutual funds. These reports are usually available in your local library or from your brokerage firm.

100

What is the difference between preferred stock and regular stock?

Preferred stock and common stock are issued by companies to investors who wish to own part of the company. Preferred stock holders get preference in payment of dividends and in case of bankruptcy or dissolution of the company. Preferred stocks normally pay a fixed interest or dividend; their prices vary inversely with interest rates. An exception is when a preferred stock is convertible into the common stock. Then, there will be more of a direct relationship between the price of the common and the price of the preferred stock. Both preferred stock holders and common stock holders have voting rights.

101

What stocks do you recommend that I buy?

It would be presumptuous for me or any other investment advisor to recommend specific investments to you without knowing anything about you. Unless I know your personal background; your name; if you are single, married, divorced or widowed; number of dependents, your occupation, annual income and investment objectives, I couldn't begin to recommend a stock to you.

In addition to making specific recommendations, I need to know your investment experience, level of expectations, the types of investments you have and your tolerance for risk. Also, what is the value of your assets? Retirement assets? Debts (including mortgages)? Is there anything unique about your situation? Any health concerns? Legal concerns? Potential inheritances or proceeds for sale of a business or practice? Obviously if you won a $25 million lottery last year and it is payable over 20 years, your financial situation will have changed dramatically.

These are only some of the reasons why investments that are appropriate for some people are completely inappropriate for others. When a complete stranger telephones you and tries to sell you an investment without discovering first if it suits your needs, you should politely say "no thank you" and end the conversation.

102

What is the Dow Jones Average? I hear it mentioned on evening news and I don't understand it.

The Dow Jones Average is an index of 65 stocks. These 65 stocks, (30 of which are in the industrial category) are large companies such as General Electric, Coca Cola, AT&T, General Motors, DuPont, and Merck. Twenty transportation stocks and 15 utility stocks are also included — for a total of 65 stocks.

The Dow Jones Industrial Average is the only price-weighted index commonly reported. This means that movements of higher-priced stock affect this average more.

The 15-stock index of the Dow Jones Utilities will give you additional insight because utilities need to borrow more heavily than to finance their capital-intensive operations. That's why this index is such an effective barometer of interest rates.

103

What are the various indices listed in the financial section of the newspaper? What do they mean?

◆ The most commonly quoted index is the **Dow Jones Industrial Average** (Symbol DJII). Thirty of the largest blue chip common stocks traded on the Big Board (NY Stock Exchange) comprise the Dow Jones Industrial Average.

◆ **The Standard & Poor 500** (S&P 500) consist of 500 large capitalization stocks. The S&P 500 symbol is SPX. This is the gauge used by most portfolio managers to compare and measure their performance.

◆ **Dow Jones Transportation Average** (symbol DJIT) is used to track 20 large transportation common stocks.

◆ **Dow Jones Utilities Average** (symbol DJIU) tracks 15 utilities stocks.

◆ **American Stock Exchange** (symbol AMEX) is the third largest stock exchange in the United States. This index tracks stocks on this exchange.

◆ **NASDAQ Composite Index** (symbol COMP) consists of smaller, usually more volatile companies traded on NASDAQ's National Market System.

◆ **Wilshire 5,000** (symbol WSX) offers the most comprehensive view because it tracks all major NYSE, AMEX and NASDAQ stocks.

◆ The index for foreign stocks is **The Morgan Stanley Capital International Europe Australia Far East Index** (Symbol EAFE). It tracks 1,080 stocks in 20 countries.

104

What stocks make up the Dow Jones Averages?

The Dow Jones Averages consist of 30 industrial companies (the Dow Jones Industrial Average), 20 transportation companies (the Dow Jones Transport Averages) and 15 utility companies (the Dow Jones Utilities Average). The breakdown (as of 7-97) is as follows:

Industrials	Transports	Utilities
Union Carbide	Yellow Corp.	American Electric Power
IBM	Alaska Air	Williams Companies
Aluminum Co. of America	XTRA Corp.	Columbia Gas
Caterpillar	CNF Transportation	Unicom Corp.
DuPont	Caliber Systems Inc.	Enron Corp.
Coca-Cola	Delta Air Lines	Public Service Enterprise
International Paper	UAL Corp.	Peco Energy
Merck	APL Ltd.	Consolidated Edison
American Express	Norfolk Southern	Consolidated Natural Gas
Procter & Gamble	CSX Corp.	Edison International
Boeing	Federal Express	Pacific Gas & Electric
Walt Disney	Burlington Northern	Noram Energy
Eastman Kodak	Ryder System	Duke Power
Philip Morris	AMR Corp.	Southern Co.
McDonald's	Conrail Inc.	Texas Utilities
Chevron	Union Pacific	
United Technologies	Airborne Freight	
Minnesota Mining	Southwest Airlines	
General Electric	US Airways	
Exxon	Illinois Central Corp.	
AT&T		
Johnson & Johnson		
Travelers		
Sears Roebuck		
Hewlett-Packard		
AlliedSignal		
J.P. Morgan		
General Motors		
Goodyear		
Wal-Mart		

105

I've added the values of the 30 stocks making up the Dow Jones Industrial Average. That sum was around 2200, which doesn't equal the average. How is the Dow Jones Industrial Average calculated every day?

By adding each day the prices of the 30 stocks when the New York Stock Exchange closes at 4:00 p.m. Eastern Standard Time. (The composite prices, which are reached only after all the other exchanges have closed later in the day, are not included.)

Then divide that total from the current divisor, .33098002. This divisor is less than 1 because of the many splits that have occurred among the stocks of the Dow Jones Industrial Averages. The divisor is adjusted every time the stock of one of the 30 companies splits or whenever stocks are added or dropped from the average.

106

When should I sell a stock?

This is a common question that has no simple answer. When to sell a stock depends upon your investment objectives. Many people buy a stock and have no idea when they plan to sell it. In other words, they really have no investment goal. What happens is: the stock goes up and they don't want to sell it because they'll have to pay capital gains tax on it. Then, the stock starts to drop below the purchase price, causing great concern. They don't want to sell the stock then because they'll have a loss. So they decide to wait until it rises up to break-even and then at that point they plan to sell it. What happens? The stock continues to drop below the lows and reaches new lows.

For fear of paying the tax on the capital gain, these investors have missed a profit opportunity and incurred a loss.

This loss could also have been avoided through the use of a stop loss order. You determine at the time you purchase a stock that if it drops 10-15% below the purchase price, it is automatically sold. So, by having a selling discipline in place, you will limit your loss. As stocks starts to rise and reach new highs, you keep reestablishing your selling discipline to 15% below the new high and when it reaches that new low, the stock is automatically sold. This is one method of locking in a profit and not riding a stock without a plan.

107

What does P/E mean? I see it in the paper when I look up my stocks.

P/E stands for the price-earnings ratio. To calculate the P/E for a particular company, divide the market price of one share of stock by the annual earnings of one share of stock. For example, if the market price of a specific stock is $30 and the earnings per share are $3, then the P/E = 10.

Investors use the P/E ratio as a yardstick in evaluating a company's comparative worth. Some analysts recommend buying stocks with low P/E ratios because they may be undervalued. Stocks with greater future earnings growth prospects usually sell at higher P/E ratios. It's a good idea to understand what P/E is and realize it is one of many measures to use when deciding whether to invest in a particular company.

108

What is the difference between the "bid" and "asked" prices I see in the stock quotation listings in any local newspaper?

The *bid* is the highest price an investor is willing to pay for the same security. The *asked* is the lowest price at which an investor is willing to sell a security at a specific time.

Bid and *asked* confuses many investors. To avoid confusion, rephrase them as, respectively, "What can I buy it for?" and "What can I sell it for?"

109

What is the origin of the stock market terms bear and bull?

In 18th century England, bear skin traders frequently sold their skins before they had actually caught them. *Bears* came to refer to speculators who sold shares they did not own; hoping for a price drop. They would then buy the stock after it had fallen and would immediately sell it for a higher price. *Bull* probably came to mean the opposite of *bear.*

110

What is the difference between a market correction and a bear market?

How bad it gets. Both involve stock market drops. A correction is a slump of 10%-20%. A bear market is a stock market drop of 20% or more. True long term investors shrug off a market drop as a temporary condition which will turn around at some point. Those same investors get a bonus: Their reinvested dividends buy a lot more shares.

111

How is the market cap for a company calculated?

The market capitalization of a company is calculated by multiplying the market price per share times the number of shares the company has issued. If a company has issued 10 million shares and the market price is $25, then the market capitalization = $250 million (10 million x $25).

As a general rule of thumb, the stocks of larger capitalization companies are considered less volatile and easier to sell at the price you want. The smaller the capitalization of a company, the more volatile its stock price and the harder it is to sell at the price you want.

Analysts view capitalization as one criteria to consider when selecting stocks. They define a large cap stock as more than $5 billion, a midcap as $1 billion-5 billion, small cap as $250 million to $1 billion, and micro cap under $250 million.

112

Why have my utility stocks lagged the market?

Utility stocks are very interest rate-sensitive. Because they borrow heavily to finance their operations as interest rates go up, the value of utility stocks tends to go down, because they have historically, paid a higher percentage of dividends than other stocks do. During the time you mentioned, there had been six increases in interest rates; that had adversely affected the value of utility stocks.

113

Florida Power and Light (FPL) cut my dividend by 34%. Is there any indicator that could have alerted me in advance? I don't have a broker.

One of the indicators that is commonly used to warn investors that a company is going to cut the dividend is that the dividend becomes greater than the earnings of the company. When the dividends of the utilities are approaching 90% or more of its earnings, that dividend may be in danger of being reduced or eliminated. This was the case with FPL.

114

How can I time the stock market just right?

Trying to time the stock market is something that you should avoid. Historically, it has been proven that individuals cannot time the stock market well. It's much more important in order to get a high return on your investments over the long term, and to have the proper asset allocation. The proper asset allocation has counted for 91% of investment returns — whereas market timing has only accounted for 2-3%.

115

How can I tell when the market is going to correct so that I get out in time?

Don't try. Guessing which way the market will move in the short term is generally a loser's game. The Dalbar Group of Boston did a 10-year study of stock investors in 1994. Those investors achieved an 80% return while the Standard & Poor's 500 increased almost 300%. Why? The investor's returns were much lower because they tried to time the market and did it badly — as most investors do. It's time in the market that makes investors succeed, not timing the market.

116

Do you recommend reinvesting the dividends I receive from blue chip stocks I own?

Definitely. The return you get by reinvesting dividends is much greater than you get by receiving cash dividends. The Standard & Poor's Composite Index of 500 widely held common stocks (commonly know as the S&P 500) has increased more than 400% during the past 15 years. If dividends from these stocks had been being reinvested in purchasing additional shares during this period, the return would have soared to 851%.

117

What is dollar cost averaging?

Dollar cost averaging invests a fixed dollar amount in a particular security or mutual fund on a regular basis. For example, an individual may be investing $500 a month into a mutual fund. When the price of the fund drops, that $500 buys even more shares. Dollar cost averaging is also known as the Constant Dollar Plan.

118

Any drawbacks to dollar cost averaging?

Dollar cost averaging is a strategy designed to eliminate the ups and downs of the market. However, you'll be penalized in a steadily rising market. Why? Each time you buy, you get fewer shares than the last time.

119

Is dollar cost averaging strictly for small investors depositing $50-100 a month into a fund?

No. An individual investing $120,000 into a variable annuity may not want to risk buying into the market for fear that it's too high. Instead of investing $120,000 at one time, then seeing the market drop, the investor could use a different approach. In this dollar cost averaging method, the first $120,000 is deposited into a money market account inside the variable annuity. Then, each month $10,000 ($\frac{1}{12}$ of the total) is automatically transferred for investment into an equity account inside the annuity. After 12 months that $120,000 is fully invested.

120

How do analysts evaluate a stock? How accurate are they?

Analysts evaluate stocks by examining the earnings of a company and its prospects for the future. They also analyze the prospects for growth for the industry and economy, and look at the historical data of the company's finances. They may meet with the company's management and discuss its growth and operations to get a feel for the effectiveness of its leadership. Some analysts meet with the company's competition, suppliers, customers and clients, and look for trends within the industry as well as the company. It is crucial that the analysts study the demand for the company's products or services (both domestically and overseas) so that they can accurately forecast growth prospects. In addition, they must have thorough understanding of the company's finances, profit margins, and areas for improvement.

Analysts who are not accurate in their predictions usually

have to change jobs because they're replaced. Analysts stick out their necks by making forecasts and predictions, in black and white, in written reports. They are held accountable.

121

What is the difference between a limit order and market order?

A **limit order** specifies the highest price you are willing to pay for a stock, or the lowest price you will accept for the sale of a stock you own. If you make a **market order**, you are not specifying a price; your order will be executed for the best price available at the time you place the order. You'll learn the price after the order has been executed.

122

How can I capture gains on appreciated stocks by using "stops"?

By using a stop order to sell you can capture profits or limit losses on the stocks you own. For example, you buy 100 shares of a stock at $40 and wish to limit possible losses in case the stock plunges. You establish your stop loss at 85% of the market price or at $34.

Suppose the stock rises steadily from 40 to 50s, and then on to 60. While it is rising, you should be adjusting your stop loss accordingly (market price x 0.85) as shown below.

market price	$40	50	60
stop sell price	34	42½	51

After the stock price peaks at $60, the market goes through a correction and stock price eventually drops to 38. When the price dropped to $51, your stop loss order was activated automatically. This stop loss strategy enabled you to lock in an $11 share gain ($51 sell price — $40 cost price).

Remember, a stop order becomes a market order once a specific price is reached or penetrated. This excellent strategy eliminates the emotional pressures of investment decisions. Don't expect your broker to call when the stock gets close to a stop price, asking you if you want to change it. This would defeat the objectivity of this risk reduction approach.

123

What is the difference between "technical analysis" and "fundamental analysis" in evaluating stocks?

Fundamental analysis studies the basics of a company's finances and its economic prospects before making a decision to buy, hold, or sell its stock. Fundamental analysis studies a company's prime earnings ratios, dividend history, rate of return (or equity), sales, and profitability history and trends.

Technical analysis uses past and current stock price movements to predict future prices of a company's stock. It relies heavily on charts to plot the price movement of stocks. No consideration is given to any of the components used in fundamental analysis.

124

Several financial magazines have praised the "Dogs of the Dow Theory" for investing. What is it?

The "Dogs of the Dow Theory" also called the "Select 10 Portfolio" consists of the top 10 yielding companies of the 30 in the Dow Jones Industrial Average. Remember:

$$\text{Yield} = \frac{\text{Dividend}}{\text{Market Price}}$$

This formula means that yield will go up when a stock's price goes down. When the market price of these blue chips drops, their yield goes up. Because these Dow stocks are out of favor, they have been nicknamed *The Dogs of the Dow*. Historically, investing in the Dogs of the Dow has produced annual returns of 18.08% a year during the last 25 years, ending in 1996. Compare that result to 12.76% for the Dow in general and 12.35% for the S&P 500 for the same period. This approach also dramatically beats the returns on the S&P index funds.

125

What are defensive stocks?

Defensive stocks are stocks that are less vulnerable to the swings of the business cycle than most other stocks tend to be. Some defensive stocks include utilities, household products, and food stocks. They are considered defensive because consumers need to buy these products or services regardless of changes in their personal incomes or job situation.

126

Should I invest in retail company stocks?

Your question is very general and, while there are many dynamic retail corporations, there are also retailers who have either been unable to find their markets or have lost them. An excellent way to judge retail sales is to make a "same-store sales comparison." To do this, you need to compare sales at stores that have been open for at least one year. By looking only at stores that have been open for a year or more, you eliminate the effects of increased sales caused by recent new store openings.

When analyzing a manufacturing company, use comparative unit sales rather than dollar sales to get a better indicator of demand for the company's products.

127

What common mistakes do stock fund investors make?

Many investors are attracted to mutual funds because it means you can hire a professional manager, sell your shares easily and instantly diversify your portfolio.

They, and you, can make several mistakes. The first is putting your money into several funds within the same sector. If you do, then you have duplicated or maybe even triplicated your portfolio. When that sector is going down, you've got a triple disaster.

Another common mistake is betting on last year's top funds. Top performers rarely repeat. If you're going to invest in mutual funds, you must be willing to stick with your investment for at least five years. Remember, terrific performance may be synonymous with terrific volatility.

By the way, timing the market, even in mutual funds, is a big mistake — one which participants in 401(k) retirement plans are making all to often. So are professional managers. In January 1995, several of them thought the stock market was considerably overpriced. They cashed in most of their holdings and waited for the market to fall. It didn't. Fully invested individuals reaped the benefit as the stock market kept going up; followers of the money managers didn't.

There is an easy formula for avoiding all these mistakes: Buy quality, invest for the long term, be well diversified, be patient.

128

How can I follow my stock holdings in the newspaper?

Let's assume you own AT&T and have the Wall St. Journal.
Refer to Section C, Money & Investing, to find the New York
Stock Exchange Composite Transaction. You'll find the fol-
lowing for AT&T.

52 week						Vol					
Hi	Low	Stock	Sym	Div	Yld%	PE	100s	Hi	Lo	Close	Net Chg
s44-1/8	31-5/8	AT&T	T	1.32	3.7	10	34329	36-1/8	34-3/4	35-1/4	-3/4
A	B		C	D	E	F	G	H			I

A = "s" indicates stock recently split

AB = highest and lowest prices stock traded during last 52 weeks

C = Sym is stock symbol

D = Div is annual dividend per share paid in cash to shareholders

E = Yld is annual dividend divided by market price of stock

F = PE means Price Earnings Ratio which is the market price of a share of stock dividend by its earnings per share

G = 100s is number of shares (in blocks of 100) that traded on the prior trading day

H = Hi-Lo is highest and lowest price paid for the stock on prior business day

I = Net Change in stock price up (+) or down (-) from the close of the prior trading day

Chapter 6

Understanding Bonds

Many investors view bonds and bond mutual funds as conservative investments that provide a steady income and represent a minimal risk to principal. That's because if you hold your bond until maturity, you get the full amount of your investment plus interest. (A bond is an obligation of its issuer to pay the interest and principal as promised.)

Zero-coupon bonds are very popular among parents and grandparents who are funding a child's education. A zero-coupon bond is issued at a discount from its par value (or face value). It only pays interest with principal at maturity or at the time the bond is called. Unlike other types of bonds, interest on zero-coupon bonds is not paid to you every six months; it is automatically reinvested or compounded at the agreed-upon rate at time of purchase. The combination of compounding and the discounted price means that a relatively small investment can multiply significantly before the bond matures. The longer the maturity length of the bond, the deeper the discount usually is.

In addition to being used to fund a college education, zero-coupon bonds appeal to many individual investors who are planning for retirement. If placed in SEPs, IRAs or Keoghs, they are not subject to immediate taxation since these accounts are tax-deferred. By making an investment in a zero-coupon bond today, investors know exactly how much they will receive at maturity.

Municipal bonds are debt securities issued by public authorities (such as states or municipalities) to raise funds for building or repairing schools, highways, prisons, bridges, tunnels and other public works. The interest payments you receive on municipal bonds is free from federal income taxes. The higher your tax bracket, the more you will benefit by investing in "munis" and earning tax-free income.

If you live in a high income tax state you may also derive additional benefits from owning in-state bonds that are also exempt from state income taxes. Interest on bonds issued by the U.S. Virgin Islands, Guam and the Commonwealth of Puerto Rico is exempt from federal, state and local taxes in all fifty states. **Corporate bonds** complement many investment portfolios — especially retirement accounts and accounts with low marginal tax rates.

Many reputable companies raise capital by issuing corporate bonds to purchase or update equipment, build plants, and replace outstanding debt with lower cost issues. Credit rating agencies such as Moody's and Standard & Poor's (S&P) study the creditworthiness of the issuer of the bond, and assign a rating to that bond as a general guideline for investors. Investment grade ratings used by agencies are:

Moody's	S&P
Aaa	AAA
Aa	AA
A	A
Baa	BBB

These agencies revise their ratings when they feel the creditworthiness of an issue changes.

United States government securities are among the most secure of all income-producing investments. They are available in two forms: direct obligations of the U. S. Government and those issued by various agencies which are indirect obligations of the U.S. Government.

All bonds (U.S. Treasuries, federal agencies, zero-coupons, corporates and municipals) are subject to market fluctuations if you sell them before they mature.

Investing in bonds has become more complex in recent years as the choice of taxable and tax-exempt bonds has expanded and volatility in bond prices and interest rates has increased.

129

How do bonds work?

When a bond is issued by a corporation or a municipality, it is sold at face value. The investor usually pays $1,000 per bond. The par value also includes the amount that will be redeemed or repaid at maturity. To calculate the market price of a bond, use the following formula:

current yield = amount of coupon/market price.

If a 6% bond is issued at par or $1,000, the amount of coupon interest = $60 or

$$.06 = \frac{\$60}{\$1000}.$$

Let's assume the Federal Reserve raises interest rates in order to reduce inflationary pressures. The yield on bonds goes to 8% and the market price is reduced.

current yield = amount of coupon/market price

current yield = .08

coupon (remains constant) = $60

market price =   X

$$.08 = \frac{\$60}{X}; \quad .08\,X = \$60; \quad X = \frac{\$60}{.08};$$

X = $750 market price

When interest rates are lowered, the market price of a bond increases. Let's assume the Federal Reserve lowers interest rates to stimulate the economy. The yield on bonds drops from 6% to 5% and affects the market price.

current yield = amount of coupon/market price

current yield = .05

coupon = $60

$$.05 = \frac{\$60}{X}$$ X = $1,200 market price

130

I'm 68 years old and I understand the benefit of investing in insured tax-free municipal bonds. But are there any disadvantages?

Yes, there are three disadvantages; *market risk, inflation risk* and *call risk.* The principal of these bonds is only guaranteed upon maturity.

◆ If you wish to sell them before maturity and interest rates have gone up considerably since you've purchased them, you will find that the principal is less than the purchase price, and you will be taking a loss if you sell them. This is *market risk.*

◆ If you hold tax-free bonds until maturity, the money you get back (even though it is equal to the face-value of the bonds) has lost purchasing power over the years because of inflation. Bonds that you've held for thirty years may only have 25% of the purchasing power they had when you purchased them. This is *inflation risk.*

◆ When interest rates drop, the issuer of your bonds may wish to call or redeem them and refinance them at a lower rate. This is *call risk.*

131

How can I know whether I'm better off investing in taxable or tax-free bonds?

By computing whether the return net of taxes is greater than tax-free versus tax or vice versa. How do you do this? There is a formula for computing the tax equivalent. Take your tax-free return percentage-wise, divide it by one minus your income tax bracket. That will give you the tax equivalent. Let's assume somebody has a six percent tax-free investment and is in the forty percent tax bracket. Put 6% in the numerator and then (1-.40) in the denominator (so you have $.06/.60$). The answer is .10 or 10%. So, the 6% tax free bond would be the equivalent of 10% before taxes (if an investor is in the 40% bracket).

$$\text{Tax Equivalent Yield (TEY)} = \frac{\text{Tax-free return}}{1 - \text{income tax bracket}}$$

$$\text{TEY} = \frac{.06}{-1 - .40}$$

$$\text{TEY} = \frac{.06}{.60}$$

$$\text{TEY} = .1 \text{ or } 10\%$$

132

Is there any risk associated with investing in CDs?

CDs (certificates of deposit) are insured by the Federal Deposit Insurance Corporation (FDIC). There is no risk of default on the principal of a CD, but there is risk that the value of the CD will diminish through loss of purchasing power. Remember, the only true value money has is by measuring the value of the items it can buy. If the value of the items an investment can buy is reduced, then there is a risk of inflation. Many retirees are frustrated when their CDs or bonds come due and the amount of purchasing power has been reduced by inflation.

133

Is there a rating service for bonds (similar to Morningstar Ratings for mutual funds and Value Line for stocks)?

There are three rating services: Moodys, Standard & Poor's and Fitch. The highest rating is AAA, then AA, A , BBB, BB and B for investment grade quality. When a municipality pays to insure their bonds, their credit rating is enhanced and becomes AAA.

134

What are mortgage-backed bonds?

Mortgage-backed bonds or collateralized mortgage obligations (CMOs) are pools of mortgages repurchased by the agencies that issue them. Some of these agencies are better known by their nicknames:

- ◆ **Ginnie Mae** stands for Government National Mortgage Association (GNMA)
- ◆ **Freddie Mac** stands for Federal Home Loan Mortgage Corporation (FHLMC)
- ◆ **Fannie Mae** stands for Federal National Mortgage Association (FNMA). Each payment the investor receives is for interest only until the return of principal payments begin.

135

What is a money-market account? How does it differ from an account at a bank? Can you write checks against it?

A money-market account is not *guaranteed* by the brokerage firm from which you buy it. There is no fluctuation of principal. The interest rate is, in almost all cases, considerably higher than is found at a bank. Many brokerage firms offer accounts that enable owners to write checks against their account.

136

Am I better off investing in registered or book-entry municipal bonds? Can you purchase the same bond either way? Is there a price difference?

Most municipal bonds are issued in book-entry form only. You are probably better off buying book-entry municipal bonds because, that way, you will not have to worry about losing your certificates. A bond cannot be purchased both in book-entry and registered form. They are only issued in one form or the other.

137

I am retired and have recently changed my residence from New York to Florida. Does it make sense for me to "swap" or exchange my New York municipal bonds for Florida ones?

Compare your New York municipal bonds with those available in Florida, and see if the return justifies the swap. If your return in New York is equal to your potential return on a Florida bond, then the additional Florida Intangible Tax may make it worthwhile for you to "swap" into Florida municipal bonds.

138

What is a callable bond?

When interest rates drop, an issuer (usually a corporation or municipality) may wish to redeem its outstanding bonds and refinance them at a lower rate. It's similar to an individual refinancing a home mortgage when interest rates drop considerably since the date the mortgage was issued. Bonds with call provisions protect investors from having their bonds called or redeemed before a specified date (such as 5 or 10 year call protection).

139

What does "laddering a portfolio" mean?

Laddering is a strategy for protection against interest rate risk when buying tax-free or taxable bonds that have different maturities. Think of a portfolio with bonds that have varying maturities as resembling rungs of a ladder. By purchasing bonds that mature at set intervals, the investor has diversified in case of changes in interest rates. In addition the investor can plan for income and reinvest principal at set intervals.

140

On cable TV they talk a lot about the yield curve being normal or inverted. What does this mean and why is it important?

A yield curve is a graph that plots interest rates for a security that is issued with different maturity lengths. Yield curves can be plotted for municipal bonds, corporate bonds and treasury securities. (Interest rate is measured on the vertical axis and the time period on the horizontal axis.)

The yield curve that is generally referred to on TV is the yield curve for Treasury securities. It usually slopes upward because interest rates are higher as maturity lengths increase. This is what is called a *positive* or *normal* yield curve.

When short-term interest rates shoot up because of inflation fears, the yield curve slopes downward because longer-term maturities have lower rates. The yield curve in this scenario is called *inverted.*

In rare instances, short-term and long-term interest rates are almost equal. The yield curve is then called *flat.*

141

What does "secondary market" mean?

After a stock is issued in an initial public offering (referred to as an "IPO"), its shares may be sold and bought again and again. The "again and again" constitutes the secondary market.

142

Does a T-bill differ from a treasury note? A treasury bond? Or are they all the same?

A T-bill (Treasury bill) is a short-term obligation of the U.S. Government. They have maturity lengths of one year or less, are purchased at a discount and mature at face value. At maturity (either 13, 26, or 52 weeks), the difference between your purchase price and maturity value is considered taxable interest income.

Treasury notes and Treasury bonds are also U.S. Government obligations but have longer maturities. The maturities are:

◆ Treasury notes: 2-10 years
◆ Treasury bonds: more than 10-30 years

Both Treasury notes and Treasury bonds pay interest every six months and are issued in $1,000 denominations. When financial broadcasters refer to the interest of the *long bond,* they mean the 30-year U.S. Treasury bond.

Chapter 7

Paying For College

In the last twenty years, the cost of a college education has increased at more than double the rate of inflation. In some Ivy League schools, alumni children are literally paying more for one semester's tuition than their parents paid for four years' tuition thirty years ago.

If you start an educational funding investment plan when your child or grandchild is an infant, it will be much less of a strain on your finances. To begin formulating your investment plan, you need to calculate how much it will cost and how much you will need to invest (either in one lump sum or annually). Most major brokerage firms have computer programs designed to determine the cost for college educations for up to four children in a family. These programs usually have a selection of 1,700 or so colleges and universities, their associated four-year costs and historic annual increases.

A growing number of people have postponed starting a family until they were in their 40s. Instead of funding their retirement plans, they are now paying college bills *and* may also be providing support for elderly parents. Although it can represent a financial challenge to fund a child's education, most people realize the importance of doing so: studies have shown that a college education can help boost lifetime income by $1 million.

143

What investments do you recommend for funding a college education?

A lot depends upon the age of the people involved. The proper investment needs to be determined by the time horizon and the risk tolerance of the investor. If the future college student is one or two years away from entering college, then the time horizon is quite short. You would have less risk investing in more liquid investments with low volatility so that the principal would be available in the next one or two years when the money is needed.

If a child is five years or more away from entering college, you will want this investment to have more growth benefits and would therefore likely select either a mutual fund, common stocks, or even a zero-coupon bond.

144

I am worried about being able to afford to pay for a college education for my children (ages 3 and 5). How can I estimate the costs and be able to pay for them?

The first part of your question deals with estimating the costs of a four-year college education for your two children starting in thirteen and fifteen years, respectively. We know the approximate current costs of a four-year college for a private college, state university, and expensive private colleges. Based upon the past, we can also estimate the annual increase for tuition and room and board. College costs have increased at more than twice the rate of the Consumer Price Index. Based upon this increase, I would estimate the annual increase at 8%.

To calculate an estimate, let's assume college costs (tuition, room and board, and other expenses) are $6,500 at a public college. An easy way to compute this is to use a pocket calculator that has a memory. First, put 1.08 into the memory (to reflect the total amount of tuition each year including the annual increase of 8%). Then multiply the starting cost of $6,500 times memory recall (MR) or 1.08 and that will give you the total cost in 13 and 15 years by pressing MR 13 and 15 times. Remember, this is a rough estimate because we're relying only upon historical data.

145

Is there a way for me to pay for my grandson's college education without having to pay the gift tax? His tuition costs more than $10,000 yearly.

Yes. We know that the annual gift tax exclusion per person is limited to $10,000, but we also know that the cost of college can be $20,000-30,000. If you pay this tuition by giving your grandson the money, and then he pays the tuition, you will have a gift tax obligation. But you can legally circumvent the $10,000 gift tax limitation by paying your grandson's college tuition directly to the university or college.

But this does not cover the costs for room and board and transportation. If you wish to pay for your grandson's room and board and transportation costs, this will come out of the $10,000 gift tax exclusion.

In the same way, you can pay for someone's medical expenses or hospital expenses by paying the medical provider (whether it's a hospital or doctor) directly. That way, if the bill comes to more than $10,000, and you pay it directly you have a non-gift tax event. This is one of the rare instances that the IRS allows us to have our cake and eat it too.

146

Are pre-paid college tuition plans a good investment? Did I do the right thing by enrolling my two children in the Florida Prepaid Tuition Plan?

That depends upon certain factors. Currently, 23 states (including Florida) have prepaid college tuition plans. Prepaid tuition plans are an excellent way for parents and grandparents to provide for a child's college education. Without these plans, many families would not be able to provide a college education for their children.

The Florida Prepaid College Tuition Plan covers the cost for tuition and room and board at Florida public universities, colleges, and junior colleges. It does not cover the cost of tuition at private universities in Florida, or at public universities and colleges outside of the state of Florida.

What would happen if your two children who are enrolled in the Florida Prepaid Tuition Plan decide to go to college outside of Florida or at a private university within Florida (such as the University of Miami)? They'll receive either 1) a refund that is equal to the amount of money put into the plan plus 5% annual increases, or 2) the cost of tuition currently at a Florida public university (whichever is less).

It's safe to say that you could have probably received a much better return over the long run than 5%. The cost of college tuition has increased at approximately double the Consumer Price Index (CPI) 8-10%. If you had known that your children were planning to go to an out-of-state university, you would have been better off investing in a growth mutual fund. In that case, the Florida Prepaid Tuition Plan was definitely not a good investment. However, if your children plan to go to college in Florida and you want to lock in the cost of tuition increases, this can be an excellent investment.

If your child is enrolled in this plan and decides not to go to college, your money is refunded without interest — a bad investment.

Chapter **8**

Insurance and Taxes

Taxes and inflation reduce your real rate of return. Together, they can destroy an investor's dream of providing a college education for children, buying a home for the family or enjoying a comfortable retirement. By using tax-deferred investments such as IRAs, SEPs, annuities and 401(k) or 403(b) plans; your investments are able to compound faster over time. Protect your earning power by having disability insurance, and protect your assets from being depleted to pay nursing home care costs by having long term care insurance.

147

How much life insurance should I buy?

The amount of life insurance you should buy depends upon your current assets and your financial obligations. In rare cases (such as in the case of people who are very wealthy and have everything they need), a person may require no insurance to provide protection for their families. Many wealthy individuals buy life insurance policies to provide funds to pay their estate taxes. Most people with young children need insurance so that these children will be provided for until they're adults.

How much life insurance do you need? That's usually a compromise between the amount of money that you are able to afford and the amount of insurance protection you need. Usually very young people with small children and limited means can maximize the amount of life insurance by buying term insurance so that their children and spouse are protected.

You may have heard the story about the carpenter who had only one tool: a hammer. He saw every problem or opportunity as a nail. If you ask a full time life insurance agent how much life insurance you should buy, you'll probably get a much different answer from mine.

148

What do you recommend I do to reduce the amount of taxes
I have to pay?

Some tax planning strategies that taxpayers use to legally reduce the amount of their tax bill include:

◆ Invest in tax-free investments like municipal bonds.
Interest income from these bonds is exempt from federal income tax, and may also be exempt from state
and local income taxes.

◆ Use a home equity loan to finance major expenses such
as college education and home remodelling. Interest
expense for home equity loans are tax deductible even
if that home is not your primary residence.

◆ Pay expenses with pre-tax dollars rather than after-tax
dollars, if your employer offers flexible spending and
a 401(k) or 403(b) retirement plan. Non-profit organizations offer 403(b) plans.

◆ Shift income and deductions from one year to the next
to achieve a reduced taxable income level. For example, the only medical expenses that are deductible
are those that exceed 7.5% of income. You may be in
a position to schedule elective surgery so that it falls
within the year when your medical expenses exceed
7.5%.

◆ Rather than making cash donations to charities, do-
nate appreciated assets. By doing this you avoid the
capital gains tax on the appreciated portion and are
permitted to deduct the total amount of your donation.
For example, if a stock originally bought for $200 has
grown in value to $1,000, then when you sold it for
$1,000, you would have $800 in gain subject to the
current capital gains tax. However, if you donated this

stock (worth $1,000) to a legitimate charity, you would have no tax liability and would be eligible for a $1,000 deduction from your income tax.

◆ Sell securities with a loss to offset securities already sold with a gain.

◆ Contribute up to $ 2,000 to an Individual Retirement Account (IRA) if you are not covered by a retirement plan at work. This amount should increase to $4,000 if you have a non-working spouse. The amount of the IRA contribution is deducted from your taxable income.

◆ Investing in tax deferred investments (such as annuities) permits earnings in subsequent years to grow faster because they are not subject to income taxes — as long as they are sheltered in that annuity. Earnings accrue tax-deferred until they are redeemed.

149

How can I reduce the chances of being audited by the IRS?

Odds are you won't be, but odds are no guarantee. Your probability that the IRS will audit you is about 1 out of 100 if you file as an individual, 5 out of 100 if you're self employed filing Schedule C.

The first way to reduce chances of an audit is having your tax return prepared by a professional. Second, you must report all income. Cross-check the amount you report with the amounts reported by employers, brokerage firms, banks, and lending institutions. If you forget to report the same income these organizations report on Form 1099, the IRS computer probably will flag the return for further investigation. Third, sometimes people hear from the IRS because they overlooked small things. Two of the most common are not signing your return and switching Social Security numbers with your spouse.

Be aware that if you have a deduction outside what the IRS considers to be the normal range, the agency's computer probably will notice. Don't skip a deduction out of fear. If you or your family member have large medical or other legitimate deductions and can justify them, don't be afraid to itemize these deductions — and can justify them — take the deduction. Even if the IRS does audit you, being able to substantiate those deductions will leave your return unchanged.

150

Should I buy long term care insurance now? Or wait until I'm 65?

If, in the future, you become uninsurable because you develop an unforeseen medical condition, then you will have taken an unnecessary risk. Let's look at the real cost of waiting by examining and comparing the real cost for a benefit if an individual enrolls at age 55 versus enrolling at a later age.

The $100 benefit at age 55 will increase (due to inflationary pressure) to $130 in five years and to $170 in ten years. The total cost is much less if this policy is purchased at age 55. Aside from the economic benefits, think of the peace of mind you'll have knowing that your assets will not be depleted to pay for your long term care.

151

Should I buy flood insurance even if I am not required to do so by law? I own my home free and clear and don't have a mortgage company or bank requiring me to buy flood insurance.

If you live in either a flood- or earthquake-prone area, you need to buy the proper insurance *or* be prepared to face the consequences of being uninsured. Before Hurricane Andrew struck south Florida in August 1992, many retirees who had paid off their mortgages had no longer been required to carry flood insurance. These retirees felt that the cost for these premiums was an escapable cost because it had been about 30 years since the last destructive hurricane. Some of these uninsured homeowners in Homestead and South Miami suffered massive damage and lost their uninsured homes.

Many homeowners purchased insurance policies that paid only depreciated costs — not replacement costs. A 10-year old couch that originally cost $1,000 depreciates to $100, and its replacement cost is $1,500. How much will an insurance company reimburse even if the couch is totally destroyed? For a replacement cost policy, insurance will pay $1,500. For a depreciated cost policy, it will only pay $100.

152

What is an annuity?

An annuity is a contract sold by an insurance company to an individual. It provides payments to the purchaser (usually during retirement).

By investing in annuities, 100% of your money works for you because you receive both interest earned and interest on the portion that would have gone for taxes.

A *fixed annuity* earns a set rate of return. A *variable-rate annuity* earnings fluctuates depending upon the value of the investments.

If you cash in an annuity before $59\frac{1}{2}$, you incur the same penalties as you would have if you had cashed an IRA in before age $59\frac{1}{2}$: 10% penalty plus income taxes owed.

Think of a variable annuity as a mutual fund that is permitted to grow tax-sheltered. You do not receive an annual 1099 form on the earnings of your variable annuity. You pay taxes when you decide to receive this money. You are not required to receive a certain distribution amount at age $70\frac{1}{2}$ as you would be with an IRA.

153

Is the Maximum Anniversary Benefit offered by variable annuities legitimate?

Yes. This feature insures that the highest value achieved by a variable annuity in a given year will be paid to the beneficiaries when the owner dies. It doesn't matter how much the market drops after reaching that high point.

For example, suppose an individual invested $50,000 in a variable annuity with a maximum anniversary benefit. Then suppose the value of this annuity grew to $191,000. Then the market corrected sharply, lowering the value of the annuity to $150,000 and the owner died.

How much would the beneficiary receive? Not the $150,000, but the maximum anniversary value of $191,000.

154

Do I need to have disability insurance?

Disability insurance pays you a monthly income if you become unable to work as a result of sickness or injury. It is estimated that a 40-year old is four times more likely to become disabled than to die. However, most 40-year olds with life insurance coverage are not protected by disability insurance.

The premium for your disability insurance policy is determined by your age, sex, occupation, medical history and the amount of coverage desired. Those in certain occupations are required to pay a higher premium; those in others (such as law enforcement) are usually not insurable.

More expensive disability policies are usually non-cancelable. Insurance companies define "disabled" as not being able to perform your own occupation and not having any related occupation.

155

What is a deferred annuity and how does it differ from CDs, bonds, and mutual funds?

Banks issue CDs, corporations or governments issue bonds, investment companies issue mutual funds, and insurance companies issue tax-deferred annuities. A tax-deferred annuity is a contract with an insurance company with whom you invest a specific amount of money — either in one lump sum or periodically. At a future date of choice (usually after you retire), you start to withdraw the money. You select a plan that allows you to stipulate the amount and frequency of your income distributions.

156

My company offers a flex-spending medical benefits program and I haven't enrolled because I was told if I don't use the amount deducted I lose it. Can you explain this?

Flexible spending accounts are offered usually by large corporations as part of employee health benefit programs. It enables members to use pre-tax dollars to pay for medical and/or child care or dependent expenses. Medical expenses that are not covered by health insurance (because of deductibles, co-payments, or because such items excluded such as dental prescription glasses, contact lenses, braces, and some other expenses) are covered by flexible spending accounts. What you are doing is using flexible pre-tax income to pay for items that would normally be paid using after-tax income.

Chapter

Wills

It is estimated that two thirds of American adults do not have wills. This forces the state or courts to appoint guardians for their minor children and decide who will receive their assets after their death.

Many people fail to prepare wills because it is easier to postpone a seemingly unpleasant task than face the reality of their mortality. We have a basic conflict in our society: when asked, most people say they want to go to heaven but they also don't want to die.

By preparing a will, you will ensure that your personal goals are met for the disposition of your assets. Your peace of mind is your immediate reward.

157

If a mother remarries and dies without a will, do her children inherit part of her estate?

Her biological children from a previous marriage may get nothing and the new spouse gets it all, under the law in some states. To prove the point, read the following letter from Ann Landers, who graciously allowed me to reprint it and her response. This letter starkly shows one reason why you need a valid will.

Dear Ann Landers:

My father died without a will, so his entire estate went to my stepmother. This woman, who was almost a stranger to me ended up being the sole beneficiary of all his assets two months after the wedding. She had a child of her own, so this boy is now heir to my father's estate.

Even as I mourn him, I can't for the life of me understand why I was left absolutely nothing. How could he have been so irresponsible as not to leave a will? The fact that he didn't think to look out for me is devastating. —Heartsick in Kentucky

Dear Kentucky:

How sad. But perhaps you will find solace in knowing your letter is going to remind millions of parents to write a will now.

Permission granted by Ann Landers/Creators Syndicate

158

What problems do I create if I die without a will?

Many. Generally a valid will avoids numerous expenses and delays — as well as a lot of red tape — at a fraction of the time and cost. If you die without a valid will, here are some of the disasters which can follow:

♦ The court must appoint a bonded executor and administrator; obviously the costs are deducted from your estate.

♦ If you die before your spouse, he or she may only receive a child's share of the estate. That share may not be enough to live on. And it gets worse. The court may appoint a bonded guardian. If that happens, your estate pays the costs. Again, your heirs get less.

♦ If you and your spouse die or become incapacitated simultaneously, a judge will have to decide who gets to raise your child or children. The person the judge appoints may be someone you'd never approve. Even so, your offspring will have to live with the judge's decision.

To avoid these and many other preventable problems, one of the first questions I ask prospective clients is "Do you have a will?" I also encourage couples who want to marry to go to a lawyer and get valid wills before their wedding.

159

What is meant by "probate"?

A probate proceeding validates your will before a court. It is used to determine whether you really signed your will and whether you were competent at that time to do so.

160

What are the costs of probate?

As a general rule-of-thumb, many estate planners estimate that 5% of the value of assets cover the costs for executor, attorney, appraiser and accountant's fees.

161

Can I avoid probate?

Some methods used to avoid probate include:

◆ Hold your assets in joint tenancy. The ownership of the assets passes automatically to the surviving joint tenant.
◆ Life insurance that is not payable to an estate generally bypasses probate administration (but not estate taxes).
◆ Revocable living trusts protect the assets in that trust from being subjected to probate administration at time of death. This saves executor and attorney fees, and offers privacy about inheritances.
◆ Gifts made before death avoid probate.

162

How much will I need to pay in federal estate taxes?

At the time this book goes to press, federal estate taxes apply only to estates that are valued in excess of $600,000. This tax increases proportionally from 39% to 55% on estates greater than $3,000,000. There is a 5% surcharge on estates between $10-$21,000,000.

163

When must estate taxes be paid? May tangible assets (such as real estate) be used to pay them?

Estate taxes must generally be paid in cash within nine months of death. If market conditions are less than favorable, a forced sale could result in severe financial sacrifice.

164

Does it ever make sense to refuse an inheritance?

Sometimes. The first question to ask yourself is whether you need the money. If you don't, you may be better off disclaiming an inheritance, especially if inheriting an asset will create an estate tax situation which you could avoid.

For example suppose you were left a business worth $100,000. If that business is a gas station or has land with toxic waste and has an Environmental Protection Agency (EPA) liability of several million dollars, you have a problem because the liability is much greater than the worth of the business. That liability could taint your estate. You have a lot more to lose than gain by claiming this inheritance.

You may also want to consider turning down an inheritance you don't need if it would create estate taxes. If the inheritance went straight to your heirs, then they would get it sooner and it would be undiluted by any taxes on your estate. However, just because you refuse an inheritance doesn't mean your heirs automatically get it. I recommend that you talk to a competent estate planning lawyer before you disclaim an inheritance.

165

What information should I leave for my heirs in addition to my will?

You may wish to leave a special letter of instruction for them, as well as a farewell letter explaining your wishes and giving advice to your loved ones.

You may also wish to include instructions to help them wrap up your personal affairs (such as the location of important documents, tax returns, safe deposit boxes, credit cards, outstanding loans, insurance policies, Social Security number, military honorable discharge papers, special details about your personal effects, property deeds, or matters pending litigation). This is an excellent way for you to tie up any loose ends. Any preferences you have regarding funeral and burial arrangements can be communicated in this letter. Your letter of instruction is an excellent way to say goodbye to those you love.

166

Are life insurance proceeds included in computing estate taxes?

Yes. Life insurance proceeds are used in computing estate taxes. However, proceeds not payable to an estate generally bypass probate administration.

167

Congress is talking about getting rid of the inheritance tax. Do you think it will be repealed?

Repealing the estate tax, or keeping it, is a political decision. That means many specific interest groups will apply pressure on Congress, probably too many for it to pass meaningful legislation.

The government does make money on the inheritance tax, but not a lot. It's estimated that the government pays out two dollars collecting the estate tax for every three dollars the tax brings in. You can legally reduce or eliminate your estate's inheritance taxes if you use proper estate planning. Remember, the estate tax applies to only 1% of the population.

168

If I have a joint account (with rights of survivorship) with my adult daughter and I funded the account, do I need her signature on a stock certificate in order to sell it?

Even though all the money in this account was deposited by you, you still need your daughter's signature to sell any stock held in that account. If you and your daughter owned a home jointly and you decided to sell it, both of your signatures would be required. The same principle holds true for ownership of securities in joint accounts.

169

I am a 78 years old retired physician with three sons ages 43, 45 and 49. My oldest and youngest sons have successful careers and are in good financial shape. My middle son, however, is a credit card junkie who spends more than he makes and makes only the minimum monthly payment on what he owes. The 18-24% credit card interest is putting him further and further into debt and he's not likely to get out. He has no savings, no retirement assets, and I doubt that he ever will. I'd like to help him out and provide for him, but know he'll squander any inheritance. What do I do?

Sadly, your situation is more common than you think. Frequently adult children have medical or emotional problems from which they need protection.

I know you don't like the idea of protecting your child from himself, but you have to do what needs to be done. In this case, you need to meet with a competent estate planning attorney to create a trust for your middle son's benefit.

When you are creating this trust, here's a tip: Don't designate one or both of his brothers as trustees. Instead, pick a trust company at a bank or brokerage firm to take over as trustee when you die or become incompetent. You'll sidestep two problems that way. First, you'll avoid conflict between brothers which could ruin their relationship. Second, you won't have to worry about who the trustee will be if your middle son outlives his brothers. You can set up the trust for any number of purposes. For example, you could have the trust pay your son's medical insurance premiums, plus his mortgage or rent payments. You could even have payments sent directly to the insurance company and bank. That way your son won't have the money, so he won't be tempted to spend it on something else. In addition, you will have made sure your son will have medical care if he gets sick and a place to live for the rest of his life.

That's more security than many people have in life.

If you're going to use a bank or brokerage firm as trustee, make sure it has a good investment track record. The money in the trust has to be invested so that, on average, it grows more every year than it pays out. For example, if the trust grows 9% and only pays out 7% for your son's needs, the trust will never run out of money.

170

My sister was a widow. When she died, her three children argued constantly with each other while trying to settle her estate. Now they hardly speak to each other. I very much want to make sure that my family and other heirs do not battle with each other. Any ideas on how to do that?

No matter what your age, the death of your last parent is one of the most emotionally wrenching times you or anyone else will endure. Many brothers and sisters whose relationship was harmonious up until that point find themselves arguing bitterly over their parent's assets. Those arguments have been known to permanently and painfully damage relationships.

To avoid the kind of pitched battles you fear, talk to a competent estate planning lawyer in order to prepare a valid will. Share your concerns with the attorney.

You can prevent a lot of arguments by specifying in your will who gets each valuable asset, whether they are pieces of jewelry, works of art, stocks, bonds, or anything else. If your will spells out who gets what, then your heirs won't have any questions about what your wishes were. Don't let what you're doing take them by surprise after you've died. Bring this delicate issue out in the open. Talk to your children in a friendly family meeting so they'll know what your wishes are and understand why you are doing what you're doing.

Chapter 10

Home Ownership

Buying a home used to be the largest single invest-ment confronting most people. Many baby boomers have discovered that paying for private college edu-cations for their two or three children has eclipsed the cost of purchasing a home. When these same individuals calculate the amount they need to invest for a comfortable retirement that is likely to span thirty plus years, they are shocked to discover it exceeds the combined costs of paying for their home *and* their children's college educations.

Because of these conflicting demands, some people have decided to rent rather then buy homes and invest what they save in growth mutual funds and seek to obtain a greater re-turn on their money.

Hundreds of years ago — before the industrial revolution and the existence of factories — people worked out of their homes. Now again, in the information and telecommunications age, many Americans no longer work in downtown or suburban office complexes. They are able to work at home, linked to the workplace by computers, modems, and faxes. We seem to be going full circle.

171

Is buying a house a sound investment strategy?

Buying a home is an excellent idea — if you plan to make that home your primary residence. This should be the reason you buy a house — not because it's a good investment.

Home prices usually increase at the rate of inflation. Many home buyers have had trouble selling their homes at a profit during the last four years. The federal government encourages Americans to own their own homes by making interest payments for mortgages and property tax payments tax deductible.

172

How can I save on my mortgage?

There are several ways to save on your mortgage if you are willing and able (unlike most homeowners) to pay more in the near term to realize major savings in the long term.

By paying your loan over 15 years instead of 30 years, you'll save considerably. Your monthly payments will be approximately 30% more, but you'll wipe out your debt in half the time. Some lenders charge $1/4$ to $1/2$% less for a 15-year mortgage.

Another way is to prepay your mortgage (if there is no penalty for doing so). If your lender permits you to pay your mortgage every two weeks, you'll pay half the monthly amount every two weeks. In the course of one year, that totals 26 payments ($26 \times 1/2 = 13$) or 13 months. Under this plan, your 30-year mortgage will be paid off in 23-24 years.

173

Do you recommend applying for a fixed- or variable-rate mortgage for my primary residence?

The answer to this question depends on where you plan to live, and your ability to make the mortgage payments to cover your closing costs. If you plan to move within a short time and interest rates are low, a variable rate mortgage is probably best. If interest rates are low and you lock in a fixed-rate mortgage at that low rate, then as interest rates start to go up, your low rate will not be raised.

On the other hand, consider whether your annual income is likely to increase significantly? If so, you are in a better position of affording increased monthly mortgage payments in later years.

174

My daughter recently divorced. She has a lot of credit card debt costing 18% a year. She wants to take out an 11% equity loan on her home to pay off her credit cards. Does this strategy make sense financially?

The answer is yes — if your daughter can stick to the plan. The problem isn't when people eliminate credit card debt by taking out home equity loans. The problem comes when people cave in to temptation and start using credit cards again to buy things they don't need. Then they have both the home loan and the credit card debt to pay off. If you can't make the home loan payments, you could lose your house.

175

Do you think I should invest in raw land?

Without knowing anything about your portfolio, your risk tolerance and your investment objectives, it would be unwise for any financial advisor to advise you. Raw land is a real estate investment that offers no benefit from either income or depreciation. It only offers the benefit of possible appreciation.

Real estate, however, can be one of many investments in a diversified portfolio. We've heard stories of individuals investing in raw land that suddenly multiplies in value when oil or some precious mineral is discovered on it, or when a major shopping center developer purchases it.

176

What is a reverse mortgage?

With a reverse mortgage, you get to live in your house for the rest of your life — and the bank sends a monthly check. Yes, you read that correctly: The bank pays you while you continue living in your house.

This is a deal that works best for retirees who have lots of equity in their homes but not a lot of other assets. It provides a monthly income.

Here's how a reverse mortgage works: You make a deal with the bank or some other institution for it to buy your house, gradually. The bank sends you a monthly check. The down side is that, with every payment, you lose a small portion of your ownership in the house. The plus side is that you have cash to live on. And there's a bonus. That monthly payment is considered loan proceeds, not income, so it's tax-free. The deal ends when you die. Then the bank takes title and sells the house.

Remember, if you want to pass your house to the family or someone else, then a reverse mortgage with a bank or other institution won't work. You can have a reverse mortgage between relatives, but that's tricky. Talk to a competent estate planning lawyer if you want to consider such a move. For further information on reverse mortgages, call Fannie Mae at 800-732-6643.

177

How can I make sure my credit reports are accurate? Can I get a copy of my own credit report.

Yes. I suggest you check your credit report yearly because mistakes can and do occur. In addition, stolen or unauthorized use of credit cards and charge cards can damage your credit rating. Also, mistakes are caused by confusion created by individuals with the same name.

To order your credit report, you can call any of these three major credit reporting agencies.

◆ Experian (formerly TRW) 800-682-7654
   P.O. Box 2104
   Allen, TX 75013-2104
   $8 for credit report

◆ TransUnion (610-685-1111)
   P.O. Box 390
   Springfield, PA 19064
   http://www.tuc.com

◆ Equifax (770-612-3200)
   P.O. Box 740241
   Atlanta, GA 30374
   http://www.equifax.com

178

My wallet was stolen and my credit cards were used fraudulently. How can I protect my credit?

You can prevent fraud from ruining your credit. You just have to be prepared. To minimize the damage from being a credit card fraud victim, you need to know your credit card account numbers. Have them ready by making a list of those numbers, along with your driver's license and long distance phone card. If you tend to put off making such lists, just photocopy every card and ID that's important to you. Whichever method you use, store the information somewhere away from your wallet.

If you discover that you are a credit fraud victim, report it to Trans Union Fraud Victim Assistance Department (800) 680-7289. Give the people there your account numbers and other information they may request.

You should see several results as a result of calling Trans Union. First fraudulent accounts should be deleted from your credit file. Second, a protective statement should be placed in your credit file until you ask that it be taken out. Finally, your payment history should be corrected to adjust for whatever fraud problems may come up.

Stay alert for fraud by reading your mail closely. Watch for unusual purchases on your credit card and phone bill. Be suspicious if you are notified you've been approved for a credit card you never applied for. Watch out if you receive collection agency letters dunning you for purchases you never made or referring to accounts you don't have.

If any of these things happen to you, immediately report the credit card fraud. Send a registered letter, return receipt requested, to all of the major credit reporting agencies. Please refer to 177 for these addresses.

Finally, use an ounce of prevention: Never put your Social Security number on checks. Someone who has that number and other information about you can get additional bank cards, charge cards and bank accounts, all of them in your name.

Index
(Chapter-Question No.)

Contact Author Form
Questions and Comments

Fax: (954) 561-6569

Write: Steven Camp
            P.O. Box 11779
            Fort Lauderdale, Florida 33339-9930

Telephone: (954) 561-6515

My questions and/or comments are:

_____

_____

_____

_____

_____

_____

Your Name _____

Address _____

City _____ State _____ ZIP _____

Telephone _____

(Please photocopy)

Order Form

Telephone Orders: Call 1 (800) 356-9315

Please have your American Express, Discover, Visa or Mastercard ready.

Postal Orders: Trunkey Publishing Company
2841 NE 21 Court
Fort Lauderdale, FL 33305-3617

Please send *MONEY MATTERS MADE EASY*

Company Name: _____

Name _____

Address _____

City _____ State _____ ZIP _____

Telephone (_____) _____

Retail Price: $12.95

Shipping / Handling Charges:
Add $3.00 for first book and $1.00 for each additional book ordered.
For faster delivery, Priority Mail, add $4.00 for first book and $1.00
for each additional book.

Payment:
Send check payable to Trunkey Publishing Company.

Call Toll-Free and order now.

(Please photocopy)